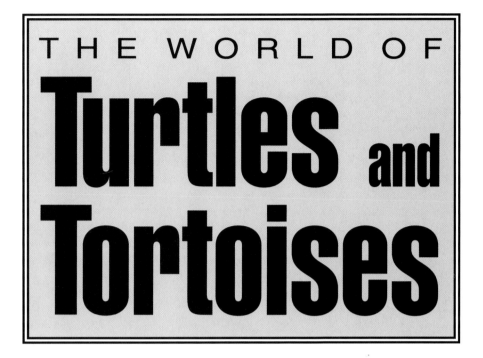

THE WORLD OF
Turtles and Tortoises

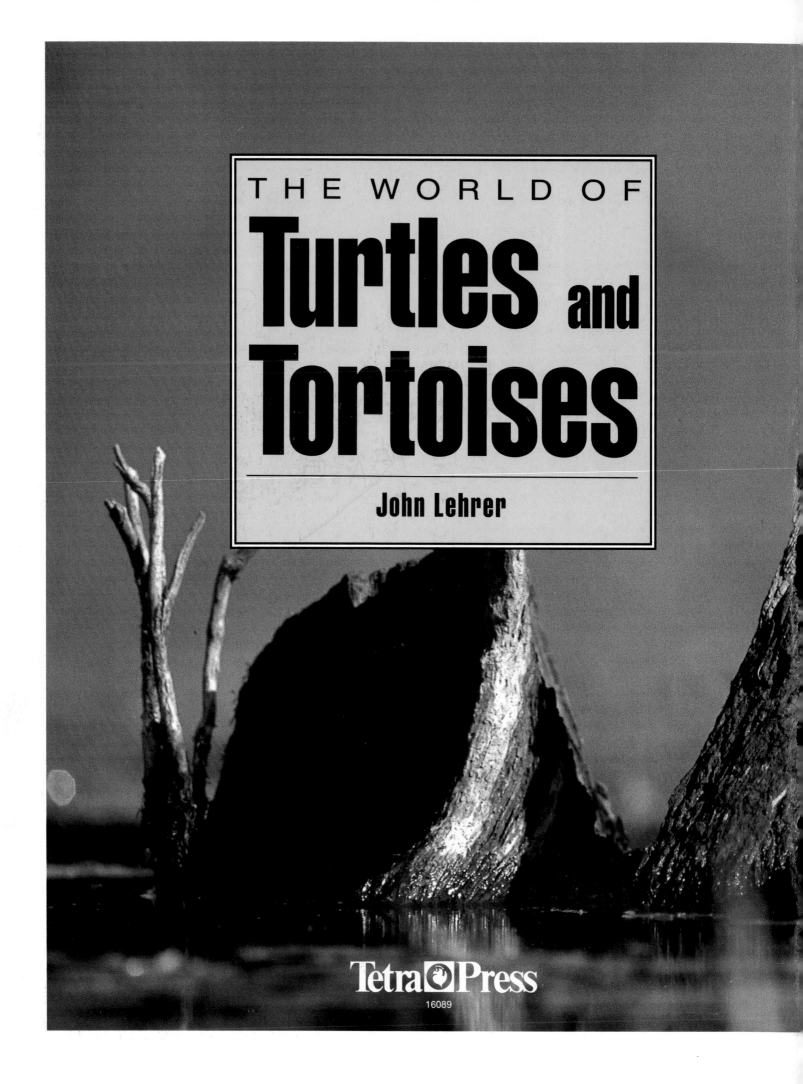

THE WORLD OF
Turtles and Tortoises

John Lehrer

Tetra✤Press

16089

A FRIEDMAN GROUP BOOK

Published in the United States by Tetra Press
3001 Commerce Street
Blacksburg, VA 24060

ISBN 1-56465-116-9

THE WORLD OF TURTLES AND TORTOISES
was prepared and produced by
Michael Friedman Publishing Group, Inc.
15 West 26th Street
New York, New York 10010

Editor: Sharon Kalman
Art Director: Jeff Batzli
Designer: Kingsley Parker
Photography Editor: Christopher C. Bain

Typeset by BPE Graphics
Color separations by Universal Colour Scanning Ltd.
Printed in Hong Kong and bound in China by
Leefung-Asco Printers Ltd.

Item No. 16089

All correspondence concerning the content of this volume
should be addressed to Tetra Press

11/94

CONTENTS

INTRODUCTION

For as long as I can remember I have been fascinated by reptiles. Like millions of other American children, I was given a baby turtle as one of my first pets—a red-eared slider, which we mistakenly called a "painted" turtle—when I was quite young. Through ignorance, I fed it fish food and kept it in a small tank with too much water and too little dry land. In a short time it died, as do most pet turtles.

When I was eight or nine I spent many summer days in my hometown of Sandusky, Ohio, roaming the banks of Pipe Creek, near a cemetery on the outskirts of town. Mostly I looked for garter snakes, which I'd take home (much to my mother's dismay) and keep in a glass-sided terrarium my father built. Occasionally, I came across adult painted turtles. I took them home, too, but later released them because I did not have an adequate place to keep them.

I read a lot as a child, and some of my relatives inadvertently encouraged my interest in reptiles: My grandmother gave me Raymond L. Ditmars' classic work, *Snakes of the World,* and a great aunt gave me Holling Clancy Holling's *Minn of the Mississippi,* which I still consider a superb book on snapping turtles.

Shortly thereafter I stopped collecting snakes and turtles, turning to more conventional pets such as cats and dogs, but I've never lost my interest or affection for this ancient class of animal. Whenever I visit a natural history museum, zoo, or pet shop, I invariably head for the reptiles first.

Though turtles, like snakes, are reptiles, somehow they have always seemed different to me and, apparently, to many others. Turtle expert Archie Carr summarized the feelings of millions when he said: "Most people have a vague feeling that no reptiles except turtles are to be trusted." I have always thought that of all the reptiles, turtles seem the most approachable and innocuous. Snakes and crocodilians, by comparison, seem slightly sinister, although no less interesting for it. As for lizards, they have always seemed to me to be misfits, an attempt at a snake that didn't quite succeed.

Yes, turtles definitely are appealing creatures. People readily develop the same sort of warm feelings for turtles otherwise reserved for hamsters, rabbits, guinea pigs, and kittens—except, of course, those people who regard turtles primarily as a source of food.

Apart from the feelings of affinity and affection they evoke, turtles are interesting because they are not quite what they seem. On land, they may be awkward and slow, but in water, the natural element for many, they are creatures of speed and grace. Similarly, the turtle's shell creates the sense that it is a simple, one-dimensional, somewhat comical creature, and throughout history the turtle has been the butt of many fables and jokes. In fact, the turtle's shell is a remarkable feat of natural engineering that, in its differing forms, has assisted the turtle in adapting to a variety of environments.

In this book I want to enlarge the reader's awareness of the complexity of this tough, adaptable animal, which has thrived on Earth for more than 150 million years. To this end, I have described in nontechnical terms the turtle's body structure and how it works, given a fairly complete overview of the various turtle families, and provided interesting details of the life patterns of many individual species. In the final chapter, I describe the complex and frequently disastrous relationships between turtles and human beings.

I have not attempted to write an exhaustive or scientific description of all facets of turtle anatomy, physiology, and behavior. Instead, I have presented the most appealing turtles here, to provide the most comprehensive overview possible. A number of books, many of which are listed in the bibliography (page 124), describe most of the known facts about the more than two hundred species of turtles.

A few words about terminology. "Turtle," "tortoise," and "terrapin" are terms commonly used to describe the subject of this book, and usage varies according to culture. For instance, the British generally use the term "turtle" to refer only to sea turtles; other shelled reptiles are referred to as tortoises.

In America, all species that are semiaquatic or fully aquatic are called turtles (for instance, painted turtles and leatherback turtles); the term "tortoise" refers to species that live primarily on land (the desert tortoise, for example). The term "terrapin," derived from a Native American word, is used primarily to mean any turtle that is sold to be eaten (referring mostly to the diamondback terrapin, but also to cooters and sliders).

Strictly speaking, however, the term "turtle" is correct when applied to any shelled reptile.

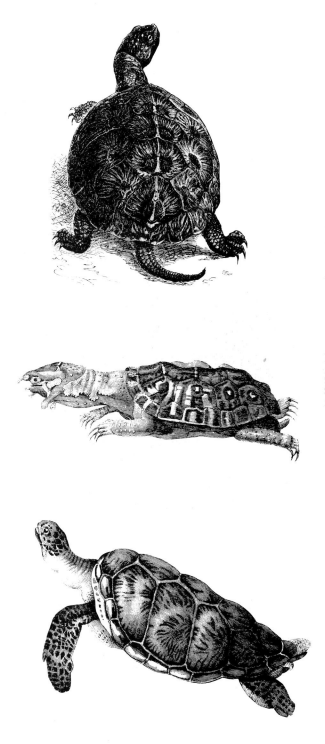

TURTLE BIOLOGY

CHAPTER ONE

What a remarkable animal is the turtle! Consider: Prototurtles evolved more than 200 million years ago, and giant ancestors of turtles shared the earth with dinosaurs during the Golden Age of Reptiles. The turtle survived the demise of the dinosaurs, and in its present form has thrived for upwards of 150 million years. That's three times as long as modern mammals and more than 3,000 times as long as *Homo sapiens* have inhabited the planet.

A turtle may be defined as a reptile with a bony or leathery shell into which its head and limbs can be partly or, in some cases, fully retracted. Turtles have no teeth; instead, they have beaklike jaws with a sharp cutting edge. Turtles have four strong legs, usually equipped with claws, suitable for walking, crawling, or swimming, plus a tail.

At first glance, human beings find turtles attractive because their shells are so prominent. For most people, a turtle is its shell; the terms become synonymous. This is both ironic and unfortunate—ironic because while in a literal sense the shell does provide protection for the turtle's internal and external body parts, it also creates a barrier, hiding the complex physiological reality of the turtle from those who find turtles interesting but inaccessible.

The shell's prominence also creates the sense that turtles are simpler and less diverse animals than they actually are. In fact, there are a dozen distinctly different major types, or families, of turtles and more than 200 species in all.

Turtles live in most of the temperate, semi-tropical, and tropical regions of the globe in almost any imaginable surroundings—woods, ponds, rivers, lakes, marshlands, prairies, deserts, and the open ocean. In the wild, most turtles are omnivorous, eating food as varied as insects, tender seagrasses, carrion, fruit, and fish. A few, however, are either carnivorous or vegetarians.

Turtles range in size from a few inches in length (the eastern mud turtle, for example, found in the eastern United States) to the largest of all turtles, a sea turtle known as the leatherback, which inhabits tropical waters and may reach nearly 8 feet (3 meters) in length and weigh as much as 1,500 pounds (560 kilograms).

If any qualities can be said to characterize turtles, then, it is their ability to adapt and to endure. Having developed a body type that suits its needs for obtaining food as well as for protecting and reproducing itself, the turtle's continued well-being on the planet is threatened only by the inconsiderate and/or wantonly destructive actions of humans.

SCIENTIFIC CLASSIFICATION AND REPTILE EVOLUTION

In order to understand how animals and plants are both similar to and different from one another, scientists categorize them according to a classification system devised by the Swedish botanist Carolus Linnaeus in the 1700s.

Linnaeus' system, consisting of nine levels (shown below), is hierarchical, meaning that the categories at the top of the list ("kingdom," "phylum") refer to the broadest and most significant distinctions among groups of plants and animals, and those categories at the bottom ("genus," "species") refer to less significant distinctions that, nevertheless, mark one animal and plant as identical to or different from another. Thus, the animal kingdom includes all animals, but the family of turtles known as Chelydridae includes only snapping turtles.

CLASSIFICATION OF THE ALLIGATOR SNAPPING TURTLE

What follows is the scientific way to categorize the largest freshwater turtle in the United States, the alligator snapper, which is found in the rivers, canals, lakes, swamps, and ponds of southern and south-central states:

Kingdom:	Animalia	All animals
Phylum:	Chordata	Animals with a notochord
Subphylum:	Vertebrata	Vertebrates (animals with backbones)
Class:	Reptilia	All reptiles
Order:	Chelonia*	All turtles (and tortoises)
Suborder:	Cryptodira	Straight-necked turtles
Family:	Chelydridae	Snapping turtles
Genus:	*Macroclemys*	Distinguished by three prominent ridges on the carapace (upper shell), extra scutes, and lateral eye placement
Species:	*temmincki*	Alligator snapping turtle

*Depending on the source consulted, the order name for turtles is either "Chelonia," "Testudinata," or "Testudines."

A common snapping turtle casts a wary eye upon an intruder into its domain.

The first significant category to pay attention to in this classification scheme is subphylum: Animals either have backbones (vertebrates) or they don't (invertebrates).

Turtles belong to the group of animals known as reptiles (Reptilia), one of five classes of animals in the world that are vertebrates. Reptiles are considered a more advanced form of vertebrate than are amphibians (Amphibia) and fish (Pisces), but less advanced than birds (Aves) and mammals (Mammalia).

As suggested earlier, contemporary reptiles are the survivors of a much more extensive group of animals that evolved from amphibians and flourished during the Mesozoic era, which lasted from about 230 million years ago until 70 million years ago.

Reptiles were the dominant form of life at this time. They ranged in size from those as small as present-day lizards to perhaps the largest animal ever to inhabit the earth, the recently discovered *Seismosaurus,* which may have reached a length of 120 feet (44 meters) and a weight of 90 tons (82 metric tons). Reptiles of this time adapted to every kind of environment—swamps, deserts, forests, grasslands, rivers, lakes, oceans, even the air.

Toward the end of the Mesozoic era, fossil evidence indicates that the dinosaurs and about 80 percent of the other living reptiles died out rather suddenly (geologically speaking) for reasons still not clearly understood. Their dominant position was taken by the higher vertebrates, birds, and mammals.

Today, reptiles still make up an important part of the animal kingdom; almost 6,000 species, mostly lizards and snakes, still exist. They help preserve the delicate balance of nature by eliminating large numbers of rodents, insects, and other pests.

Returning to the classification system, turtles are an order (one of four) within the class of reptiles; the three other living orders are snakes and lizards (Squamata); crocodiles, caimans, and alligators (Crocodilia); and the tuatara (Rhynchocephalia), a rare, lizardlike reptile that lives only on a few islands near New Zealand.

What makes reptiles different from other vertebrate classes are the following qualities, which are shared by turtles: a skin covered with scales or horny plates; a pair of lungs to breathe air; a body temperature that fluctuates with the environment; reproduction by internal fertilization; the ability to lay tough, durable eggs on land; and offspring that look and act like miniature adults.

A passing familiarity with scientific classification is all the lay person interested in turtles requires. For the purposes of this book, then, I'll make an important distinction between suborders in the section on turtle anatomy that follows and then primarily discuss different families and species of turtles, mostly using the common name rather than the Latin name for the animal.

The Florida box turtle's hinged plastron enables it to completely close itself off from the world outside.

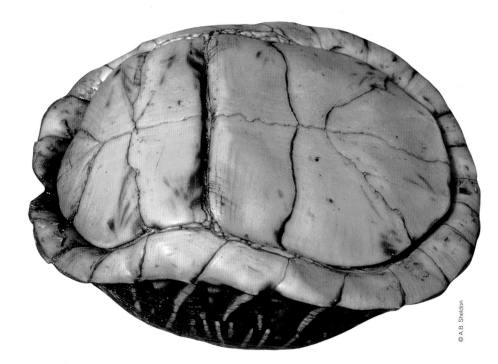

Modern turtles evolved from small animals known as cotylosaurs, or "stem" reptiles, which lived about 250 million years ago and from which all reptile lines have evolved. The first true turtles—equipped with bony or leathery shells and with a scissorlike jaw in place of teeth—appeared during the Triassic period, a little more than 200 million years ago.

During the Mesozoic era, turtles were a far more varied order than they are today. In fact, turtles were divided into three suborders, one of which is now extinct. They evolved in ways that suited their habitats, developing light, leathery shells and large, powerful legs with webbed feet for swimming, or high, domed, bony shells and elephant-like legs for living on land.

Fossil remains of early turtles have been found in Europe, North America, South America, Asia, Africa, and Australia. Many were the size of modern turtles, but some were much larger than any turtles presently living. A fossil of a tortoise shell measuring 6 feet (2 meters) in length, for instance, was found in India, and remains of sea turtles reaching nearly 11 feet (4 meters) in length were found in the United States.

Any discussion of turtle anatomy has to begin with that most obvious element of turtle architecture, the shell. Most vertebrates have an internal skeleton that is covered with muscle tissue (flesh) protected by scales, hair, feathers, or, in the case of humans, skin. Turtles are the opposite, having their skeletons on the outside of their bodies which protects the flesh and vital organs contained within. Some people have the notion that a turtle's body is contained inside the shell, and that somehow it might be possible (and easier) for the turtle to get around if only it could unburden itself of its shell. But that's not true: The shell is part and parcel of the turtle's body.

A turtle's shell has two parts: a convex dorsal (upper) section called the carapace, and a flat, belly section called the plastron. These two units are connected by bony bridges on the sides of the shell, which leave gaps at the front and back for the turtle's head, tail, and four legs to protrude.

Both the carapace and the plastron are composed of two layers. The inner layer of each consists of a mosaic of tightly joined bones. The turtle's spine is rigid, immobile, in fact, because the turtle's vertebrae and ribs have become an integral part of the inner layer of the carapace. Only the legs, neck, and tail can move.

The outer layer of the shell is made up of a symmetrical pattern of broad, horny scales (scutes). The seams of the inner and outer layers of the carapace and plastron don't coincide, which makes the integrity of the total shell much stronger.

Some species of turtles have a plastron that is hinged in one or more places. This feature allows it to flex and completely enclose the turtle's head, tail, and legs.

Turtle shells are complex and vary in their makeup from family to family; what follows is a general description of the outer layer of the carapace typical of tortoises and pond and marsh turtles, which constitute more than half the living species (see diagram).

ANCESTRAL TURTLES

CHELONIAN ANATOMY

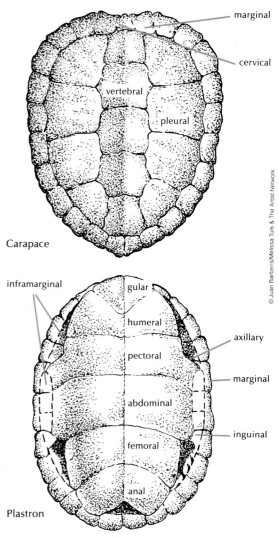

SCUTES OF THE TURTLE SHELL.

© A.B. Sheldon

Above: The symmetrically decorated plastron of a yellow-bellied turtle, a medium-sized North American emydid.
Right: This Florida soft-shelled turtle is able to lie on the bottom of a river in shallow water and stretch its neck to the surface to breathe.

© Dr. E.R. Degginger

Usually, there is a series of five large scutes running from front to back along the midline of the carapace; these are known as the vertebrals or centrals. On either side is a row of four larger scutes, known as costals or laterals. Around the edge are a series of about twenty-four smaller scutes, called marginals. Just above the head is a small scute known as the nuchal, and just above the tail is a scute termed the supracaudal.

Many modern turtles no longer require the heavy armor-plated shells their ancestors needed for protection from dinosaurs and other large reptiles. So, in the course of evolution, the shape and composition of the turtle's shell have adapted to the environment inhabited by a particular type of turtle.

For instance, it would be very difficult for a turtle to swim with a bony, heavy, high-arched shell such as tortoises possess. Sea turtles, therefore, have developed relatively sleek shells (plus broad flippers that move in breast-stroke fashion), which allow them to move rapidly through the water at speeds (for short distances) comparable to the fastest human runners.

The soft-shell turtle, such as those found in North America, has developed a shell with a flat, rounded shape that is also covered by a tough, leathery skin. This allows it to burrow easily in the soft bottoms of streams and ponds, camouflaging its body until a tasty meal appears.

Apart from its shell, the turtle's neck is probably the most interesting and significant part of its anatomy. Long and very mobile, a turtle's neck is made up of eight vertebral segments (mammals have seven).

In fact, it's the flexible nature of the neck (and the surrounding muscles and skin) that allows a turtle to pull its head back into its shell. Turtles withdraw their heads in two different ways, and this determines one of the primary methods of classifying them.

Side-necked turtles (suborder Pleurodira) withdraw their heads by pulling their necks to the side. At one time, species of Pleurodira lived in North America, Europe, Asia, South America, Africa, and Australia, but for unknown reasons became extinct. Now, side-necked turtles live only in South America, Africa, and Australia.

The dominant form of turtles in the world today belong to the suborder Cryptodira, sometimes called "straight-necked" or "hidden-necked" turtles. Turtles of this suborder pull their necks straight back into their shells. Viewed from the side, their necks take on the shape of an S-curve when withdrawn.

Several other features of the turtle's anatomy are distinctive and deserve mention. The first is the turtle's skull, which is unlike that of other reptiles and is considered primitive (meaning that it has changed very little from that of fossil turtles). Termed "anapsid," it has a solid cranium and no openings near the temples.

As has been mentioned, contemporary turtles have no teeth, though rudimentary dentition has been found in some fossil skulls. Jaw shapes vary from species to species, but most function like the blades of scissors, shearing animal flesh and plants with their sharp, horned edges.

THE NECK AND OTHER PARTS

An easy way to lose a finger: The imposing jaws of a common snapping turtle.

© Manny Rubio

A Florida gopher tortoise, which digs long burrows often shared by other creatures.

A turtle's skin is tough and scaly but flexible, especially at the neck, where wrinkles and folds allow for extension and withdrawal of the head. The legs are often covered with somewhat larger, thicker, overlapping scales for greater protection. The nails on the feet of many turtles are quite sharp and are useful for digging and climbing.

Finally, an unusual feature of chelonian anatomy is that because of the all-encompassing nature of the turtle's shell, the pectoral and pelvic limb girdles (to which the turtle's legs are attached) are within the rib cage. In most animals, they are above and below, respectively.

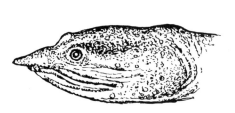

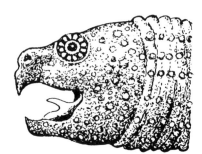

TURTLE PHYSIOLOGY

If turtle anatomy is unorthodox and fascinating, turtle physiology—the way their bodies work—is even more so.

Take, for instance, the way turtles breathe. Mammals, birds, and even other reptiles can take air into their lungs by expanding the chest cavity, but because their ribs are part of the carapace and their shells are rigid, turtles must use another method.

Turtles inhale by means of two muscles located next to the hind leg sockets, below the vital organs. When these expand, they allow air to enter the lungs, much the same way the diaphragm works in mammals. To exhale, turtles use a third, complex muscle that pushes the vital organs against the lungs, forcing the air out.

Alternative methods of breathing are necessary, however, because when a turtle senses danger and withdraws its head and legs into its shell, the air in its lungs is forced out (sometimes producing a hissing sound, which many people mistakenly interpret as a hostile gesture). If a turtle is threatened for a long period of time, it may have to survive with its lungs almost emptied of air. And what about aquatic turtles, which spend long periods of time submerged?

As it turns out, turtles do have other, less obvious ways of taking in oxygen: Some aquatic turtles are able to use their mouths as a kind of gill, drawing water in through their nasal openings, isolating and absorbing the oxygen, then expelling the water. Soft-shelled turtles are also able to absorb oxygen through their skin, and some aquatic turtles can absorb oxygen through thin-walled sacs located near their anal openings.

It may seem that these alternative breathing methods wouldn't take in much oxygen, which might be true. But turtles don't require as much oxygen as many other animals do. This has less to do with their activity levels (to think that all turtles are lethargic and slow-moving is a mistake) than with the way their bodies operate.

When most animals, including man, hold their breath for a period of time, they have to begin breathing again not so much because they lack oxygen as because they can't tolerate the buildup of carbon dioxide in their lungs. Turtles, however, are able to tolerate high levels of carbon dioxide, improving their ability to survive without breathing. Furthermore, when aquatic turtles dive, their heartbeat slows down, lowering the demand for oxygen.

This gives some turtles the ability, for example, to go for several days underwater without breathing in their normal way. In fact, the late Archie Carr, a herpetologist who spent much of his life studying

Below: Different jaw types among turtles (*left to right*): the parrotlike beak of the big-headed turtle (*Platysternon megacephalum*) of Southeast Asia; fleshy lips cover the sharp, horny jaws of a soft-shell (*Trionyx* species); the alligator snapper (*Macroclemys temminicki*) has a hooked beak for taking prey; similar to the alligator snapper, the leatherback's (*Dermochelys coriacea*) jaw also has a hooked beak for catching prey; the short, broad beak of the giant Aldabra tortoise (*Megalochelys gigantea*) is ideally shaped for chewing vegetation; the Indian roofed turtle has serrated jaws for eating water plants.

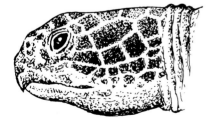

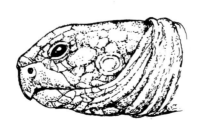

and working to preserve the sea turtle, described an instance in which a turtle survived for twenty-four hours in a container filled completely with nitrogen.

"COLD-BLOODEDNESS"

A few words should be said about turtle metabolism. Reptiles, turtles included, are often termed "cold-blooded" to contrast them with birds and mammals. However, this term is misleading.

Birds and mammals—man, for instance—are known as "endotherms," meaning that they maintain a constant body temperature, which is regulated by internal mechanisms.

Turtles and other reptiles (also fish and amphibians) are termed "ectotherms," meaning that their body temperature is much more dependent on the temperature of the surrounding environment. Ectotherms practice "behavioral temperature control," which means that they control their body temperature by seeking out or avoiding warm ground or sunlight.

Turtles take in much of the heat they need from basking in the sun; this is true for all types of turtles and tortoises, aquatic as well as those who live on land. Different species require different ranges of temperatures to thrive.

A concern with ambient temperature is less important for turtles living in tropical regions (especially forests, where variations of temperature and humidity are minimal), but it is another matter for turtles living in temperate regions. When the temperature begins to drop in early fall, many turtles prepare for several months of hibernation. This holds true even for turtles and tortoises kept as pets in places such as southern California, where the overnight temperature in midwinter rarely drops below 40°F (4°C) and the temperature at midday may be more than 70°F (21°C).

TURTLE PHYSIOLOGY

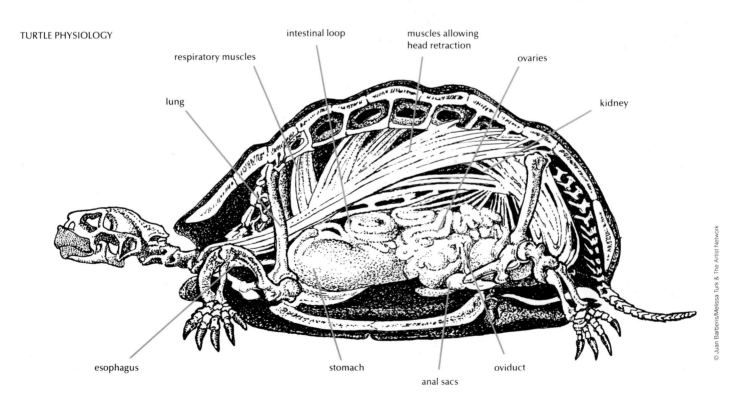

intestinal loop

muscles allowing
head retraction

respiratory muscles

ovaries

lung

kidney

esophagus

stomach

oviduct

anal sacs

Among aquatic turtles, the variety that makes its way into the northernmost waters is the leatherback; although it nests exclusively in tropical and semitropical regions, individuals have been spotted as far north as the coast of the maritime provinces of Canada.

Humans often think that because of the burden of their shells, turtles are clumsy and lead sedentary, slow-paced lives. Such a conclusion is inaccurate. Certainly the shell, which may account for one-third of a turtle's weight, must be accommodated, but most turtles are agile, strong walkers or swimmers. What they lack in speed, they make up for in endurance and persistence.

TURTLE LOCOMOTION

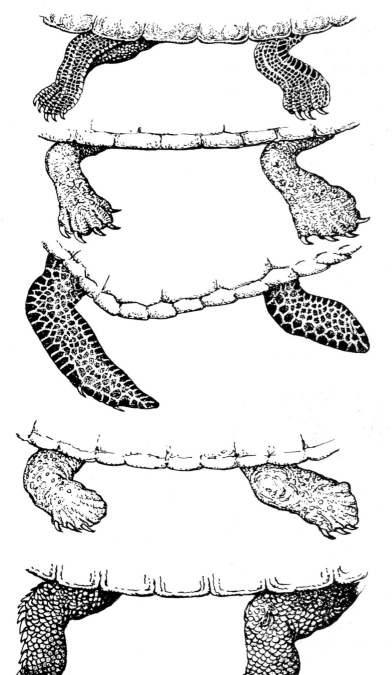

A turtle's legs and feet are shaped for its environment and style of locomotion (*top to bottom*): Pond turtles have scaled feet with well-developed claws on the front and only moderately webbed rear feet; river turtles' feet are more webbed, enabling them both to swim well and to move about on land; the front legs of sea turtles take the form of flippers and move in a breast-stroke fashion; soft-shell turtles have webbed feet with only three claws; tortoises use their flattened forelimbs to dig, while their elephantine hind legs provide sturdy support on land.

© Manny Rubio

In spite of the burden of its shell, many turtles are good climbers. Here, an African pancake tortoise descends some rocks.

How a turtle gets around depends, of course, on its habitat, and over the millions of years turtles have lived on Earth, different species have adapted well to the parts of the globe they inhabit. Different families of turtles have developed almost a half-dozen distinct varieties of limbs to assist in their movement.

The giant tortoises of the Galapagos Islands, for instance, travel from the coast to high, mountain plateaus, raising their heavy bodies off the ground as they walk. So strong are their legs and shells that they could carry the weight of a human on their backs and still continue to move along. Sea turtles, whose forelimbs have evolved into paddles or flippers, are excellent swimmers, moving through the water rapidly and gracefully. Amphibious turtles, who divide their time between land and ponds, rivers, or lakes, often have webbed feet that serve them well for walking or swimming.

Turtles use a number of different senses to carry out the primary activities of their lives: finding food, avoiding danger, and courtship and mating.

The senses of sight and smell are most important to turtles, because both are used to obtain food. The eyesight of most turtles, for instance, is quite sharp, particularly at short distances. Their long-distance vision and ability to notice different forms is good, too, even under water. Experiments have determined that turtles also can discriminate between lines of different widths and can distinguish a variety of colors: red, yellow, green, blue, and violet. They make finer distinctions among colors at the red end of the spectrum. Turtles can also distinguish different types of food by sight.

Turtles' eyes are protected by their eyelids; their eyes also have large tear ducts. This latter feature is especially noticeable in sea turtles, who "weep" when laying their eggs. This occurrence has given rise to folktales that the animals are in pain or feel sad about leaving the eggs. In fact, the tears serve to wash sand from the turtle's eyes. It is interesting to note that turtles shed tears at the same rate underwater.

Even more important than keen eyesight to the task of searching for food, however, is a turtle's sense of smell. Accomplished by means of the nostrils and (as with other reptiles) the Jacobson's organ, the sense of smell is perhaps the turtle's most efficient and powerful method of perception. The sections of the turtle's brain having to do with smell are large and well developed.

Aquatic turtles can even find food in cloudy water with their sense of smell. Also, both sea turtles and land tortoises search out and recognize potential mates, as well as other turtles of the same species, by sniffing, particularly in the anal region, where glands secrete odorous substances specific to a turtle's sex and species. Female turtles also may find their nesting grounds partly by their senses of taste and smell. Some authorities think that when a female baby sea turtle hatches on a beach, it tastes the sand, and this makes an imprint in its memory. Years later, based on that recollection, the adult sea turtle makes its way back to the same beach. (Turtles apparently have a well-developed sense of taste: They will sometimes reject food after taking a bite, perhaps indicating that they object to the way it tastes.)

It would seem that turtles can't hear well at all; at least, they're not able to easily or proficiently distinguish types of sounds from one another. Turtles have well-developed ears, although it's often difficult to determine the external location because it's frequently covered by one or more scales.

Turtles do, however, have what some sources term a "seismic" sense: They can detect low-frequency vibrations transmitted from the ground. They seem to have an accurate sense of the distance of the source of the vibration and whether it represents a danger to their well-being.

It's not clear whether turtles have voices, though some species definitely are able to make distinctive noises by exhaling, grinding, or clicking their jaws. Most vocal noises made by turtles occur during mating. The giant male Galapagos tortoises roar at five-second

SENSES, PERCEPTION, AND INTELLIGENCE

Two North American emydids: (*above*) a juvenile false map turtle, which lives in the central United States; (*below*) the abundant river cooter, which is found throughout the southern United States.

Above: A giant tortoise from Indefatigable Island in the Galapagos. These tortoises were heavily exploited for their oil until at least the 1930s, perhaps even later. *Left:* A red-eared slider, the most common pet turtle in the world.

intervals. The big-headed turtle of Southeast Asia is reputed to squeak or scream when picked up. It's probably accurate to say, however, that turtles don't communicate with each other in any significant way by means of uttered sounds.

Many turtles also display a discriminating sense of touch. For instance, a part of the courting behavior of some male painted turtles is to gently stroke the face of the female with their long claws as they swim near the females. Also, female turtles, when laying eggs, can dig a hole of the correct size and shape, as well as arrange and bury their eggs without looking at what they're doing—completely by a sense of touch.

Most humans find that clean, healthy turtles give off no odor, except for certain varieties of musk and mud turtles—known popularly as stinkpots and stinkjims—that give off a foul, musky odor as a means of self-protection, much as a skunk does. If these animals are kept as pets, they will stop giving off the odor once they've become acclimated to humans.

Are turtles intelligent? In some ways, asking such a question is pointless because it's too general and anthropocentric. What is meant by the term "intelligent," after all? Turtles are capable of amazing feats, especially where navigation and sense of direction are concerned. And something must be said for the animal's ability to adapt and survive for so many millions of years. But these qualities, admirable as they are, may have more to do with something like instinct rather than intelligence.

Turtle intelligence is not a subject that has been much studied. Experiments have shown that a turtle can learn fairly readily to slowly work its way through an elementary maze, but turtles certainly lack the sort of problem-solving abilities characteristic of mice. Similarly, it's undoubtedly futile to attempt to teach a turtle the sorts of tricks a dog might take to readily, such as "fetch," "roll over," or "play dead."

On the other hand, turtles kept in captivity respond to, and in some cases seem to recognize their owners, particularly persons responsible for feeding them. Anecdotes have been recorded of pet turtles who wait by the refrigerator at feeding time and turtles in zoos that learn when feeding time is.

In *The Running Press Book of Turtles,* author Richard Nicholls, quoting naturalist Henry Beston's *The Outermost House,* offers perhaps the most pertinent remarks about turtle intelligence:

> For the animal shall not be measured by man. In a world older and more complete than ours they move finished and complete, gifted with extensions of the senses we have lost or never attained, living by voices we shall never hear. They are not brethren, they are not underlings; they are other nations, caught with ourselves in the net of life and time, fellow prisoners of the splendour and travail of the earth.

COURTSHIP, MATING, AND REPRODUCTION

SEXUAL MATURITY AND SEXUAL DIFFERENTIATION

Among turtles, courtship, mating, and reproduction are complex and mysterious phenomena—less so, fortunately, for the turtles involved in the process than for humans attempting to understand it.

The first factor complicating the understanding of turtle sexuality is that not only do different species of turtles reach sexual maturity at different ages, the same is sometimes true for turtles of the same species.

For instance, male stinkpots, a variety of freshwater musk turtle found in North America, become sexually mature at age three or four, but females do not reach sexual maturity until their ninth to eleventh year, according to one study. (Another puts the ages at three years and two to seven years, respectively.) Male and female gopher tortoises, on the other hand, reach sexual maturity in fifteen to twenty years.

Second, because the sexual organs are internal (within the cloaca), it's sometimes difficult for a human to tell a male turtle from a female, especially if there are no distinctive secondary sexual characteristics for that species.

Especially difficult varieties to differentiate sexually include certain species of snapping turtles and tortoises. (Again, this is a problem only for humans. Turtles themselves have no difficulty in this regard.)

In general, the following external characteristics can be used to distinguish male turtles from females, though not all occur together in a single species:

Mating Galapagos tortoises. Different species of turtles have their own distinctive courtship and mating rituals.

The plastron of the female is flat, whereas that of the male may be slightly concave. This makes it easier for him to mount the female's carapace, and remain mounted during intercourse. Usually, the carapace of the female is more steeply curved and higher than that of the male.

The tail of the male is longer and thicker than that of the female. Also, the distance from the cloaca to the back edge of the plastron is greater in the male. Some male turtles have a strong horn on the tips of their tails that curves under the female's carapace during intercourse.

On many amphibious turtles, such as the red-eared slider, the front claws of the male are much longer.

It's difficult to generalize about the overall size of male versus female turtles, so this is neither an easy nor foolproof way to tell the sexes apart. In many species, the adult male and female are of about equal size. In the case of the alligator snapping turtle and some giant tortoises, the males are much bigger. In many species of painted turtles, however, the female may grow to be more than twice as large as the male. Male diamondback terrapins are also generally much smaller than females. The same is true of color. In other animals—birds, for instance—the male is generally the more brightly colored of the sexes. With turtles, males sometimes have more distinctive coloring, but the differences are generally far less marked.

COURTSHIP BEHAVIOR AND MATING

Courtship and mating for most varieties of turtles begins in the spring. Sperm has been produced in the testes of the male the previous year and stored in the epididymis over the winter. In temperate climates, where turtles are active from April through October, male turtles come out of hibernation ready to mate. In the tropics, where turtles are active year round, mating begins with the rainy season.

Female turtles, too, begin producing eggs late in the year, and ovulation starts in May or June of the following year. At this time, the eggs are 70 to 90 percent of their full size.

During mating season, female turtles usually remain in their normal habitats, and males seek them out. Some land-dwelling species may travel several miles in search of a partner; sea turtles travel much farther.

At first, a male recognizes a female of the same species by sight, but then he checks her out by sniffing her anal region, where the odorous substances she emits let him know whether he has made the right choice. This procedure is the same for aquatic turtles.

Courtship always precedes mating, and courtship rituals among turtles are varied and interesting (as with the example of the painted turtles, above).

For instance, some species of males, notably gopher tortoises, compete with other males who may be present for the interest of females by a kind of ritualized "jousting" in which the males charge one another, retract their heads, and ram each other in the flanks.

The male gopher tortoise uses the part of its plastron that projects from below the neck (termed the "gular spur") as a lever. The object is

to hook the spur under the rival's shell and overturn him, eliminating him as a competitor until he rights himself (which could take considerable time). As indicated, these fights are ritualistic, and turtles rarely injure each other.

That's not always the case, however. Some water turtles threaten each other with hissing and a menacing display of widely gaping jaws. If this doesn't suffice to frighten one or the other away, the turtles may inflict severe wounds on each other until one of them gives up and leaves the scene.

Male turtles are not always gentle with females. Some males butt females in the flanks; some bite at the female's front legs and head gently but insistently, causing the female to withdraw her head and legs, making it more difficult to close off the genital region, hence making it more accessible. Sometimes a female indicates her willingness to mate by biting back at the male.

Some box turtles and wood turtles engage in a kind of "dance" in which the male and female approach each other, face each other at a distance of a few inches, and then move their heads rhythmically in and out and from side to side, sometimes for more than an hour. Some turtles perform a variation on this ritual in which the male circles the female one or more times.

Unlike courtship rituals, mating is much more uniform: The male always mounts the female from behind. The male's tail curves underneath, and he inserts his penis (which emerges from the cloaca and is sometimes quite long) into the cloaca of the female. Aquatic turtles mate in the water, as do amphibious turtles (generally). Turtles who live on land mate either on land or in the water.

Unlike mammals and some birds (and even some lizards and snakes), turtles have no social bonds, so mating is a random act. Female turtles often mate with more than one male, and the sperm

The desert tortoise, a resident of the American Southwest. Its large, flattened forelimbs are useful for digging. Evident in this photograph is the spur the male uses in jousting. The two males charge one another and ram each other in the flanks, all in the name of courtship.

This snapping turtle has just finished digging her nest and laying her eggs. She will soon leave her nest site, never to return.

Right: A loggerhead deposits her eggs. Note the characteristic flask shape of the nest. *Far right:* This illustration clearly depicts the egg-laying process. As the egg emerges it is caught by the turtle's hind limbs and carefully lowered into the nest.

can be stored in the female's genital tract, sometimes for several years, to fertilize future clutches of eggs.

In some species, the male grips the front of the female's carapace with his front claws. Additionally, some long-necked male turtles are able to hold onto the carapace with their jaws. Because the female box turtle has such a high, domed shell, the male often falls backward and continues to mate while lying on his back, attached at the genitals. Occasionally, a male (box turtle or other species) who has fallen on his back after mating cannot right himself, and dies.

By early summer, mating reaches a peak and is completed by late summer or early fall. This is essential in temperate climates if the eggs are to mature and hatch before winter sets in.

After mating, females seek the appropriate place to dig out a nest. For sea turtles, this is sometimes a specific, distant beach to which the female must swim. Land turtles dig nests in soil, sand, or decaying piles of leaves and other organic matter.

All turtles dig the same sort of nest: Without looking, they scoop out a flask-shaped hole as deep as their fully extended hind feet and carefully lay the eggs, which emerge from the cloaca. Tortoises living in dry climates have a difficult time excavating the ground to lay eggs; to assist themselves, they have bodily reserves of water contained in twin anal sacs. In some tortoises, these sacs are large enough to fill half the body cavity. As a female tortoise is digging her nest, she can release water from these sacs all at once or a little at a time to soften the ground and make digging easier.

NEST-BUILDING AND EGG-LAYING

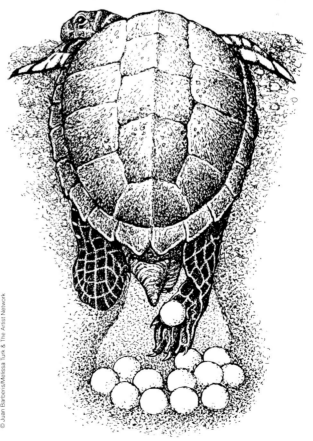

An egg emerges from the cloacal opening of a
box turtle.

© John F. O'Connor/Photo/Nats

Turtles are frequently quite oblivious to what's going on around
them while they're laying eggs. When sea turtles crawl up on the
beach and dig their nests in tropical beaches, they are sometimes
followed by food-gathering natives, who position themselves behind
the turtles and collect the eggs before they hit the sand.

After laying the eggs, the female sometimes arranges them in the
nest, then covers them with sand, soil, etc., to camouflage and
protect them. When she is finished, the female leaves the nest site,
never to return.

THE TURTLE EGG

Turtle eggs are white, but they vary according to species in size,
shape, number, shell texture, and incubation period.

Turtle eggs vary less in size than do the adult turtles from which
they come. The smallest turtle eggs are slightly smaller than an inch
(2.5 centimeters) in diameter, the largest slightly smaller than three
inches (8 centimeters).

Different species of turtles lay different numbers of eggs; some
pancake tortoises and mud turtles lay but one egg; gopher tortoises
lay up to ten; medium-sized and large land tortoises lay from ten to
thirty; and green turtles, loggerheads, and hawksbills may lay more
than 100.

These figures are generalizations: There are no reliable average
number of eggs per species, and sometimes closely related species lay
very different numbers of eggs. The largest recorded number of eggs
in a single clutch belonged to a hawksbill: 242 eggs. In general,
smaller turtles lay smaller and fewer eggs per clutch. A female may lay
from five to ten clutches of eggs per year.

Turtle eggs vary in shape from spherical (the eggs of the snapping
turtle resemble ping-pong balls) to elongated, almost cylindrical
(characteristic of certain freshwater and amphibious turtles).

In general, turtles that produce the most eggs (usually marine, river, and other large turtles) also lay soft-shelled, leathery eggs, and turtles that lay only a few eggs lay eggs with hard shells. Also, those eggs with long incubation periods (typically laid by land tortoises living in hot, dry regions) are usually hard-shelled.

Turtle eggs vary, too, in their incubation period, or the time required for them to hatch. The minimum recorded natural hatching period was thirty days for the egg of a Chinese soft-shelled turtle. For more information on incubation periods, see below.

Like all reptile eggs, the turtle egg, which has existed unchanged for 100 million years, is a complex means of nourishing and protecting the baby turtle within.

Turtle eggs have several important parts. In the center is the embryo, attached by an umbilical stalk to the yellow yolk sac, its primary food supply (composed of sugars, starches, fats, and proteins). Blood vessels in the lining of the yolk sac carry the nutrients to the abdomen of the embryo. (A sea turtle's egg is 55 percent yolk, compared to 33 percent for a hen's egg.)

The amniotic sac, an envelope filled with fluid that cushions the embryo from shock and protects it from impurities, surrounds both the embryo and the yolk. As the embryo grows it gives off waste products, which would destroy it if they were not eliminated.

INSIDE THE SHELL

A snapper deposits her eggs.

Overleaf: A common snapping turtle digging her nest.

TYPICAL INCUBATION PERIODS

Time Period	Type of Turtle or Tortoise
60 days	Wood turtles, many terrapins, Australian short-necked turtles
90 days	Snapping turtles, map turtles, painted turtles
150 days	Common Australian snake-necked turtle, gopher tortoises, Galapagos tortoises
250 days	Flat tortoises
365 days or more	African bowsprit tortoises, giant snake-necked turtles

The longest recorded incubation period was 540 days, for the egg of a leopard tortoise.

In mammals, this toxic waste is dissolved and carried away through the mother's bloodstream. In turtles, the waste is transformed into insoluble uric acid, and is stored in the allantois, a sac surrounding the embryo, yolk sac, and amniotic sac. As the embryo grows and the yolk sac shrinks, the allantois gets larger as it fills with wastes; it is also a conveyor for incoming oxygen and outgoing carbon dioxide.

A final envelope, the chorion, surrounds the allantois, amniotic sac, yolk sac, and embryo; it is a tough, resilient membrane closely associated with the eggshell that contains egg white, or albumen (40 percent of a sea turtle egg, compared to 56 percent in a hen's egg). The chorion supplies the embryo with water and some food.

By weight, the shell makes up only 5 percent of the sea turtle's egg, compared with 11 percent in a hen's egg. As these percentages suggest, the turtle's shell is thinner and semipermeable, and necessary gases and moisture are able to pass through it to the embryo inside.

SEX DETERMINATION, EARLY GROWTH, AND HATCHING

Over a number of years, different observers noticed that the ratio of females to males in natural populations and in those raised in captivity varied widely for a given species, and there was apparently no way to account for the difference.

For instance, one observer noted that 81 percent of a natural population of seventy diamondback terrapins were males; another observer noted that of 1,300 diamondbacks raised in captivity, only 19 percent were males.

Recent experiments indicate that the most important factor in determining the sex ratios of many species seems to be incubation temperature. Studies of snapping turtles, pond turtles, gopher tortoises, and mud and musk turtles reveal that if the eggs are incubated at a temperature close to either limit of the range suitable for egg development, the hatchlings will be exclusively or predominantly of the same sex.

For instance, experiments showed that for many varieties of turtles, eggs incubated at the lower acceptable temperature limit (82°F, or 27°C) produced mostly males, while those incubated at the upper limit (93°F, or 34°C) were mostly female. With other varieties, the principle remained the same, but the results were reversed. Further experiments demonstrated that the middle third of the incubation period is the critical period in which temperature determines the sex ratio of the eggs.

As might be expected, in a turtle's early embryonic development, the formation of the shell plays a dominant role. It first appears as a raised section in the back of the embryo. Called the anlage, it expands outward in every direction. As it does so, it forces the turtle's ribs to remain straight, adapting to its contours. Furthermore, the shell's development determines that the turtle's growth will be mostly sideways instead of up-and-down, the direction in which most reptiles grow. This produces the turtle's typical low, flattened body type.

As indicated, the period of incubation for turtle eggs is dependent on the genetic programming of the turtles involved, as well as on a

This series of photographs captures a Florida gopher tortoise hatching. The process may take several hours or days.

number of environmental conditions, among them temperature, humidity, and the dampness of the soil, sand, or other vegetation in the nest.

The incubation period of a nest of snapping turtle eggs, for example, may vary from fifty-five to 125 days. Assuming a period of twenty weeks, or 140 days, between the laying of the eggs and their hatching, the snapper embryo's development might proceed something like this: At four weeks the embryo is just recognizable as an animal form; by six weeks, the tail and limbs are formed and the eyes are prominent; by eight weeks, the shell is clearly recognizable. By twelve weeks, the shell is the dominant part of the snapper's anatomy, and its fingers and toes have formed. The shell is divided into shields, and pigmentation is beginning to develop. By nineteen weeks, the fully formed baby turtle, with claws and what looks to be an oversized head, is ready to hatch.

As the embryo grows into a fully developed hatchling, the shell that has offered nourishment and protection becomes a kind of prison from which the baby turtle must escape. This it does by means of an "egg tooth," which is not a tooth at all but a horny projection located on the tip of the snout. Using the egg tooth to pierce the shell, the baby turtle then pulls it apart with its forelimbs. (The egg tooth disappears as the turtle grows.)

Because all the eggs in a nest are subject to virtually the same circumstances, they all develop at very nearly the same rate. So, once a nest of eggs starts to hatch, the eggs all hatch at about the same time.

Hatching may take several hours or even days. If the weather is too cold (in temperate climates such as the United States, for example) baby turtles may remain in their eggs over the winter, hibernating, emerging in the spring.

Herpetologist Archie Carr pointed out in his classic work on sea turtles, *So Excellent A Fishe,* that baby turtles don't break loose from

BREAKING OUT

© Manny Rubio

© Manny Rubio

the nest individually. Experiments in which eggs are isolated have shown that very few turtles—perhaps one-third—break free on their own. The rest perish.

In a nest with many eggs, the hatchlings stay in the nest until a number, maybe a dozen, have hatched. Then, in what Carr terms the actions of "a simple-minded, cooperative brotherhood," the baby turtles scrape down the walls and ceiling of their nest, urging each other to break free in what amounts to a small eruption.

Once they break free, some species have a more difficult time than others. Sea turtle hatchlings, for instance, face an especially unenviable situation.

Picture the scene: a warm, tropical beach. A hundred or more tiny turtles, only a couple of inches long, break free from a sandy nest and somehow know they're supposed to scramble headlong—a hundred feet or a hundred yards—in a stampede to the sea. And in some way not fully understood, they know which direction that is.

And what's waiting for them when they break through the sand? Perhaps nothing, but that's not often the case. As Carr says, "the whole world seems against the hatchlings both during their trip from the nest to the surf and for an unknown time after they enter the sea."

Apart from humans (most of whom are interested in eggs rather than baby turtles), significant predators include dogs, buzzards,

A great many hatchlings don't make it. Animals and humans destroy countless turtle nests every year.

skunks, hawks, opossums, wild pigs, and coyotes. Many of these animals seem particularly adept at knowing when the eggs are laid and when they will hatch.

How many sea turtles make it across the beach to the surf? In many cases, certainly, a minority of those that emerge from the nest—maybe a dozen out of a hundred. And for those that make it, the safety of their first weeks and months in the ocean are threatened by gulls, large fish, and so on. All turtles face at least one additional obstacle: When they hatch, their shells are not fully hardened, making them more susceptible to predators.

Of course, many turtle nests are destroyed long before the baby turtles are ready to hatch. Because sea turtles return to the same beaches to lay eggs (and because they often show up by the hundreds or thousands), humans and other predators are there waiting to break into the nests for the turtle eggs, which they eat or extract the oil from.

The problems of sea turtle nests are not isolated, only perhaps the most well-publicized: Studies of snapping turtle nests have shown that between one-half and three-fourths are routinely destroyed, sometimes by humans but more frequently by mammals such as raccoons, opossums, dogs, wildcats, and bears.

Little is known of the first year or so of the lives of most hatchlings in the wild: They simply disappear from sight. We know that most have the capacity to go weeks or months without eating, if necessary. The next time most turtles (marine, amphibious, or land) appear in the wild is as adults a year or more old.

Most records of turtle life are based on studies of adult turtles, and most of these studies mention the absence of juvenile or adolescent turtles among adult populations. This may mean that pre-adult turtles live in different environments from those environments inhabited by adults—perhaps those offering the promise of more anonymity and protection.

This conclusion is supported, for instance, by what is known of the wood turtle's diet: Juveniles prefer meat (insects, worms, etc.), suggesting that they spend their time in the hospitable environs of marshes, bogs, and streams, where such creatures are found.

© Catherine Singer Davies

A hatchling green turtle, which died shortly after this photo was taken.

GROWTH

It's hard to accurately generalize about how rapidly turtles grow and mature. Depending on the species, turtles reach sexual maturity and full size at a variety of ages, and rates of growth are nonuniform throughout a turtle's life.

Smaller species usually reach sexual maturity and full size earliest. Male pond sliders, for instance, are sexually mature between two and five years of age; snapping turtles reach sexual maturity at six to eight years of age and continue to grow in size into their teens; common box turtles, which may live for more than 100 years, continue to grow into their twenties.

Fairly accurate records have been kept of the size and weight of many common species of turtles, but it's difficult to correlate this with a turtle's age because the life histories of very few turtles have been documented from birth.

As is the case with reptiles generally, baby turtles look and act very much like adults. However, if you were to examine a baby turtle shortly after it hatches, you'd notice two things that distinguish it from an adult. First, all baby turtles have an umbilical scar in the middle of the plastron; this looks somewhat like a human belly button, and disappears within the first year. Second, a baby turtle sometimes has a different shape, color, or different proportions from an adult of the same species.

Often, the differences are shell-related. Pancake tortoises, for example, have flat shells as adults but curved shells as juveniles. The shell of the Kemp's ridley, a sea turtle, becomes wider and wider as it matures; the shells of some adults are wider than they are long. Young leatherbacks have a mosaic pattern on their shells that completely disappears as they get older.

A turtle's shell grows from a layer of cells between the two layers of the carapace; the direction of the growth is outward from the center

Galapagos tortoises survive longer than any other member of the Testudinae family; some have been known to live for 150 years.

© Catherine Singer Davies

of each plate or scute. Close examination of the plates may reveal "growth rings" corresponding to phases of growth, much like those in trees. These sometimes become smooth and indistinct as a turtle gets older.

In some land tortoises, the shape of the shell changes with age. In many, the smooth scutes along the rim of the shell become wavy or start to flare or turn upward with age. In older painted turtles, longitudinal furrows often develop across the borders of the carapacial plates, and the "humps" or "saddles" on giant Galapagos tortoises only develop later in life.

BEHAVIOR CHANGES

From the time they hatch until they die, most of a turtle's actions are based on instinct, which might be defined as prepatterned behavior. A baby turtle never knows its mother, and although turtles are capable of learning, it would seem that they use their instinct rather than intellect in order to survive.

In captivity, groups of turtles have been observed to form themselves into a sort of primitive hierarchy in which some will defer to others; but, except for courtship and mating, most turtles have no relations with other turtles. There's no evidence that they communicate with one another or even acknowledge the existence of each other. For example, a semiaquatic turtle in an aquarium, in an effort to get where it wants to go, will attempt to climb over or swim past another turtle as if it's simply a rock or a log.

LONGEVITY

Except for the interest in a turtle's shell, people are more fascinated with a turtle's longevity than any other chelonian characteristic. It's true that given a favorable habitat and fortunate circumstances, many species of turtles live a long time.

Still, the longevity of turtles is a subject about which we have only a limited amount of information. As Archie Carr said in *Handbook of Turtles,* "The only reliable means of gaining an idea of how long turtles live is to live with them, and this of course can become monotonous in the extreme."

Emydid turtles—freshwater and semiaquatic species such as red-eared sliders, box turtles, wood turtles, map turtles, diamondback terrapins, and pond turtles—have a lifespan anywhere from twenty years (estimated, painted turtle) to forty-two years (recorded, spotted turtle) to fifty-eight (recorded, wood turtle) to 100 plus (recorded, common box turtle).

The second-largest turtle family, Testudinae (tortoises), contains some especially long-lived members: European land tortoises have been recorded to live for more than 120 years, and Galapagos tortoises have lived for more than 150 years.

In general, larger, slower-developing species have longer lifespans, but to attribute longevity to the chelonians as a whole is a mistake, the stuff of folklore and superstition: By human standards, most turtles only live a relatively short period of time.

TURTLES
—— OF THE ——
WORLD

Herpetologists don't agree completely on one single classification system for turtles. In fact, Pritchard's *Encyclopedia of Turtles,* one of the most authoritative and comprehensive works on turtles, lists six different (though not mutually exclusive) forms of classification by modern authorities. These systems separate turtles into groups based on a number of categories: order, suborder, infraorder, superfamily, and family. For our purposes, however, categorization will be more basic and relatively simple.

As stated earlier, most turtles of the world fall into the suborder Cryptodira, the distinguishing feature of which is that they draw their necks straight back into their shells. The majority of this book, and this section in particular, will be devoted to a description of straight-necked turtles.

Most authorities separate straight-necked turtles into seven distinct families: Chelydridae, snapping turtles; Kinosternidae, mud and musk turtles; Trionychidae, soft-shell turtles; Emydidae, semiaquatic turtles; Testudinidae, tortoises; Chelonidae, sea turtles; and Dermochelyidae, leatherback turtles.

Several of these families have certain characteristics in common, so in this book they will be treated as five groups: snapping, mud and musk turtles; soft-shell turtles; semiaquatic turtles; tortoises; and marine turtles (sea turtles and leatherback turtles).

A few turtles belong to the suborder Pleurodira, or side-necked turtles, which means that they lay their necks and heads sideways in the groove between the carapace and plastron (upper and lower parts of the shell). At the end of the sections on straight-necked turtles, I will describe a few of the more prominent side-necked turtles.

It's neither possible nor desirable in a book of this size and scope to describe the majority of the 200-plus species of turtles living. For readers interested in a really complete description of turtle species, I recommend *Handbook of Turtles* by Archie Carr; *Turtles of the United States* by Ernst and Barbour; *Turtles, Tortoises and Terrapins* by Fritz Obst; and *Encyclopedia of Turtles* by Peter Pritchard.

Instead, I'll discuss the turtles that are most representative of a particular family and those of a specific type that are most numerous or widespread.

The alligator snapper *(Macroclemys temmincki)* lies motionless on the bottom of streams, ponds, and lakes with its mouth open. Its tongue appears to be a red, wriggling worm, and unsuspecting fish looking for a meal become the snapper's prey.

SNAPPING, MUD, AND MUSK TURTLES

Snapping, mud, and musk turtles are grouped together because they share several characteristics: All live in the Western Hemisphere, largely in freshwater aquatic conditions (ponds, lakes, rivers, and streams); their coloration is generally unattractive and drab, and many species have aggressive temperaments.

© Dr. G.J. Chafaris

SNAPPING TURTLES

Some people think that snapping turtles are big, mean, and ugly. Well, they're big: A large common snapping turtle gets to be almost 3 feet (1 meter) long from its aggressive snout to the tip of its tail and weighs about 50 pounds (19 kilograms) (the heaviest one on record, fattened in a swill barrel, tipped the scales at 86 pounds [32 kilograms]). Alligator snappers are even bigger.

Snappers are aggressive, too. They're ready to bite right out of the egg, and their disposition worsens with age. If captured, they're initially aggressively hostile; later, they may become withdrawn, but they lose none of their meanness.

But ugly? Well, it's true that beauty is in the eye of the beholder, but snapping turtles have a kind of awe-inspiring appeal, not unlike that possessed by a heavyweight boxer or an Army tank: They're so good, so ruthlessly efficient, at what they do. And if you're smart, you don't mess with them.

The Alligator Snapping Turtle

There are two recognized species of snapping turtle: the alligator snapper (*Macroclemys temmincki*) and the common snapper (*Chelydra serpentina*). The larger of the two is the alligator snapper, which probably derives its name from the fact that the three prominent ridges on its carapace and its long tail give it an appearance similar to that of an alligator. Another source of its name may come from a folktale stating that the alligator snapper came into being when an ordinary snapping turtle mated with an alligator.

The alligator snapper is found mostly in the southern Mississippi River valley from Kansas, Missouri, Illinois, and Iowa, south to the Gulf of Mexico. It extends west into parts of Texas and Oklahoma and east, into Kentucky, Tennessee, Alabama, Georgia, and Florida. It lives, for the most part, in the deep waters of rivers, canals, and lakes.

Not much is known of the alligator snapper's behavior, but it is believed to be nocturnal and quite sedentary. It generally crawls along the bottom instead of swimming. The diet of alligator snappers is mostly meat—it

© Dr. E.R. Degginger

eats living and dead fish, frogs, snakes, turtles, crayfish, mussels, and snails—and an occasional aquatic plant.

Sometimes the alligator snapper waits in ambush for food rather than foraging for it. To do this, it makes use of one of the most unusual methods of acquiring food in the animal kingdom: The snapper lies motionless on the bottom with only its mouth open, its brownish, algae-covered shell providing the perfect camouflage. In the center of the floor of the alligator snapper's mouth is a double-ended, movable section of its tongue that looks like a wriggling, red worm. Fish are frequently attracted to this "bait" and are quickly devoured when they get within range of *Macroclemys'* hooked beak.

Except for sea turtles, the alligator snapper is the largest North American turtle and one of the largest freshwater turtles in the world. Males grow to a much greater size than females: A big male might have a shell 2 feet (60 centimeters) long, plus another foot each for the head and tail. Such a turtle could easily weigh 150 pounds (56 kilograms); alligator snappers have been recorded at more than 200 pounds (75 kilograms). Other distinctive physical features of *Macroclemys temmincki* include eyes on the side of the head that cannot be seen from directly above; a very wide head that can only be withdrawn a little way; large, bulky legs equipped with sharp claws; a similar appearance for both males and females; and a smaller plastron shaped like a cross.

Alligator snappers lay an average of about twenty-five eggs per clutch; it is thought that females may not lay eggs every year, and if they do, they lay only a single clutch. The typical lifespan for an alligator snapper is about fifty years, though some have been known to live longer. Adult alligator snappers have no enemies except man; younger turtles are probably killed by alligators, and the nests are raided by raccoons and skunks. The meat of the alligator snapper is eaten in the southern United States, though it is not as popular as that of the common snapper.

From this perspective, it's easy to see the resemblance between an alligator snapper and its namesake.

The Common Snapping Turtle

The common snapping turtle is far more abundant and has a range much greater than that of the alligator snapper. It is found all across the United States and southern Canada from the East Coast to the Rocky Mountains; it extends south into Mexico, Central America, and a few of the northern countries of South America. There are four subspecies in all; three differ in minor ways from the most prevalent, *Chelydra serpentina serpentina*.

Common snappers live mostly in bodies of water with marshy or muddy banks. They are active primarily at night; although essentially aquatic, they occasionally venture out onto land for considerable distances. When in the water, snappers usually crawl on the bottom, though they are good swimmers. Sometimes they bask half-submerged.

In the wintertime, snappers in North America burrow into the muddy bottom and hibernate. Now and again, they settle beneath submerged trees or in muskrat burrows, sometimes in large groups. By late October, most have become inactive, emerging again in March, April, or May. Apparently, common snappers tolerate cold weather fairly well; some have been seen crawling on and beneath ice.

The common snapper is omnivorous; its diet is similar to that of the alligator snapper, though it probably eats more vegetable matter, and it's quick enough to catch waterfowl from below the surface.

As is true of alligator snappers, common snappers have large, muscular legs, feet equipped with thick, sharp claws, and a long, ridged tail. Common snappers are smaller than alligator snappers, and their shells are flatter and their necks are longer. It's safe to pick up an alligator snapper by gripping it on the carapace, behind its head, but if you try that with an ordinary snapper, it will turn its head in a flash and bite your hand.

The best way to pick up any sort of snapping turtle is by its rear legs, holding the turtle far out from your body to avoid its jaws. Do not pick up a snapper by its tail—doing so will cause a potentially fatal injury to the turtle. When they're first picked up, snappers will often emit a foul-smelling musk from their tail region.

In fifteen to twenty years the hatchling snapper will approach the size of the adult.

© John F. O'Connor/PhotoNats

Above: The Florida snapping turtle *(Chelydra serpentina osceola),* a subspecies of the common snapper. *Right:* A closeup of the head of an adult common snapping turtle *(Chelydra serpentina serpentina).* Note the large, powerful claws.

Female snappers lay eggs at least once a season, sometimes more. Like the alligator snapper, the common snapper's carapace is drab in color—olive-brown, dark brown, or nearly black—and algae often grow on the shells of adults. The small plastron is tan or yellow and lacks markings.

Common snappers are extraordinarily aggressive turtles. They strike "with the speed and power of a big rattlesnake," says Archie Carr, at anything near them. This is especially true on land, where a snapper often lunges with such force that its body is lifted off the ground and carried forward.

This isn't to say that snappers seek out victims to attack. In the water, snappers are less belligerent and often prefer to escape what they perceive as danger. Snappers never become truly tame in captivity and, although hardy, make poor pets.

Snapping turtle shells had widespread ceremonial use among Native Americans, according to Carr. Snappers can be caught on fishing lines, and in North America, common snapper meat is probably the most widely eaten turtle meat and is often considered a delicacy. The eggs, too, are frequently eaten, although they will not hard-boil.

MUD AND MUSK TURTLES

The family Kinosternidae consists of small, aquatic turtles that live in North and Central America. They are known popularly as mud and musk turtles, and they number about twenty to twenty-five species in all. Most of these turtles belong to one of two genera: *Kinosternon* (mud turtles) and *Sternotherus* (musk turtles).

Most mud and musk turtles are small, having carapace lengths of 4 to 7 inches (10 to 18 centimeters); unlike snapping turtles, their tails are always short. Most species have short tubercles of barbels (projections) under their chins and on their throats. Mud and musk turtles have a hinged plastron, which allows some of them to close off their shell openings completely, protecting their head, limbs, and tail. In general, their shells are smooth, unmarked, and dark-colored (olive, brown, or black). All four of their feet are webbed.

© Dr. E. R. Degginger

There are about a dozen species of mud turtles, only a few of which will be discussed in detail. The most widespread in the United States is the common mud turtle (*Kinosternon subrubum*), which consists of three subspecies, popularly known as the eastern mud turtle, the Florida mud turtle, and the Mississippi mud turtle. Taken together, these three turtles are found mostly in the southeastern United States: South Carolina, Georgia, Alabama, Mississippi, Arkansas, Louisiana, and parts of New Jersey, Maryland, Pennsylvania, Delaware, Virginia, North Carolina, Illinois, Indiana, Kentucky, Tennessee, Oklahoma, and Texas.

The mud turtle prefers to live in shallow, slow-moving, or still bodies of water with soft bottoms, such as ponds, marshes, canals, or drainage ditches. It spends a good deal of time crawling about on the bottom, but sometimes floats near the surface and even prowls about on land. It rarely basks. On both land and water, however, mud turtles travel relatively short distances.

The common mud turtle is omnivorous, eating insects, carrion, algae, mollusks, fish, and aquatic vegetation. In winter, the species hibernates in mud, decayed wood, or vegetable debris. In the southern reaches of its range, the mud turtle remains active year round.

The razorback musk turtle *(Sternotherus carinatus)*, the largest of the genus, reaches a maximum length of about 6 inches (15 cm).

© Dr. E. R. Degginger

The striped-neck musk turtle (*Sternotherus minorpeltifer*) is a highly aquatic species living in the American South.

Nesting females show a peculiarity: They begin digging their nest with their front feet, then turn and complete it with their hind legs. They lay very few eggs, two to five are typical, and a single egg is not uncommon. Nests are relatively shallow, and the turtles make comparatively little effort to cover the eggs and conceal the nest once they are finished laying them.

The disposition of mud turtles varies; some are docile, but others are mean-tempered and bite savagely. Peter Pritchard says the most painful turtle bite he ever received was from a male Florida mud turtle. Newly captured specimens frequently emit a foul-smelling secretion. Once they become used to captivity, however, mud turtles usually cease both biting and giving off this smelly liquid. Mud turtles have a fairly long lifespan: One female, captured as an adult, lived for thirty-eight years.

Other North American mud turtles include the yellow, Sonoran, and striped mud turtles. The first two are found in the southwestern United States; the latter is found chiefly in peninsular Florida.

Another species, the white-lipped mud turtle, has a wide, entirely tropical range, and is found from Veracruz on the Gulf of Mexico south to Guatemala and northwest Colombia and Ecuador. Its appearance is distinguished most notably by the coloring of its head: The top and sides are dark brown, but the jaws and underside of the neck are white, including the upper and lower "lip" area.

White-lipped mud turtles are semiaquatic rather than aquatic. Reproduction occurs throughout the year, though females often lay only one egg. No real nest is made; sometimes the egg or eggs simply are covered with decaying leaves or vegetable matter. This variety of mud turtle is abundant throughout its range and though small (4 to 5 inches [10 to 13 centimeters] being typical), it is an important source of food in tropical Mexico and Nicaragua.

Other Central and South American mud turtles include the scorpion mud turtle and the red-cheeked mud turtle.

Musk turtles are closely related and similar in appearance and habits to mud turtles, but are generally smaller. There are fewer species of musk turtles than mud turtles, about eight in all, but they make their presence powerfully felt because of the nauseating fluid they emit from their musk glands when first handled. (Carr said: "I find the . . . musk [of the mud turtle] rather nauseating, though far from being as utterly revolting as the stench that exudes from a hysterical stink-jim.")

Additionally, many musk turtles are initially ill-tempered, scratching and biting their handler viciously. As is the case with mud turtles, however, musk turtles become quite tame in captivity.

In the United States, the most representative species is the common musk turtle (*Sternotherus odoratus*), popularly known as the stinkpot or stinkjim. It is easily identified by light stripes on the side of its head and neck. Its range extends across most of the United States east of the Mississippi River and the eastern two-thirds of Texas.

The common musk turtle is highly aquatic and, unlike the mud turtle, is frequently found in deep bodies of water. Carr observed musk turtles walking on the bottom of clear springs in Florida that were thirty feet (nine meters) deep. Other North American musk turtle species include the razorback and the loggerhead musk turtle, both of which inhabit only southern states.

Two musk turtles found in southern Mexico and Central America (genus *Stauroty-*

© A.B. Sheldon

pus), the guau turtle and crucilla turtle, are worth noting because of their relatively large size. Termed "giant" musk turtles, they are commonly a foot (30 centimeters) in length.

SOFT-SHELL TURTLES

Unlike snappers and mud and musk turtles, soft-shell turtles are predominantly fresh-water aquatic turtles found all over the world. Six genera and twenty-three species live in North America, Southeast Asia, Africa, and the Middle East.

Soft-shell turtles vary greatly in size and disposition, but many of their habits are similar, and their appearance is unmistakable. With their large, flattened, nearly circular carapaces and pointed, inquisitive-looking snouts, they seem, as Pritchard says, like animated pancakes. The family name, Trionychidae, refers not to their shells, however, but instead to the fact that soft-shell turtles have only three claws on each foot.

© John Cancalosi/Tom Stack & Associates

Above, top: A closeup of the head of the spiny soft-shell *(Trionyx spiniferus)*, the most common of North American soft-shell turtles. Soft-shells are known for their aggressiveness. *Above, bottom:* A turtle that obtains food as both a predator and scavenger, the spiny soft-shell is capable of moving quickly both on land and in water.

The Florida soft-shell
(*Trionyx ferox*), the
largest of the North
American soft-shells,
grows to a carapace
length of 20 inches (51
cm).

The term "soft-shell" is somewhat of a misnomer, for the shells of soft-shell turtles merely lack horny plates, not rigidity. The carapace of soft-shells only appears soft, because it is flat and covered with a leathery skin. The bones underneath are often quite thick; only the rim of the turtle's carapace is flexible.

The underside of soft-shells is also distinctive; in most, the plastron extends quite far forward, matching the outline of the cara-pace above or extending slightly beyond it, providing protection for the head and front limbs. At the hind feet, however, the plastron seems to be cut away, extending perhaps two-thirds the length of the carapace and leaving most of the turtle's legs and tail exposed. In most soft-shells, it is not merely the external surface of the plastron that is reduced—there are also large boneless areas in the plastron's internal structure.

Most soft-shells are highly aquatic and are

agile, strong swimmers. Typically, soft-shells have webbed feet. They have very sharp jaws, and like snappers, they strike their prey swiftly and with power. Soft-shells also are capable of moving rapidly on land: Ernst and Barbour state that a North American smooth soft-shell turtle (*Trionyx muticus*) is capable of outdistancing a human being on a level, unobstructed surface.

In general, soft-shells are medium- to large-sized turtles. At the small end of the continuum, a male smooth soft-shell, which lives in the central United States, might grow to a carapace length of 7 inches (18 centimeters); at the other end of the spectrum, the largest of the soft-shells, the Indian soft-shell (*Chitra indica*) might have a carapace length of 5 feet (1.5 meters).

As is the case with many species, female soft-shells are often considerably larger than males. One of the easiest means of differentiating the sexes is to examine the tail: Males have thick, long tails; the female's is usually short, sometimes not reaching the edge of the carapace.

Soft-shells have elongated, narrow skulls and long, flexible necks. This allows them to burrow in the mud of shallow ponds and streams, merely extending their nostrils to the surface to breathe. The skin of many soft-shells is more water permeable than that of other turtles; therefore, soft-shells are able to take in oxygen by means of gaseous exchange through the skin and lining of the throat, in addition to normal breathing. Soft-shells lack cloacal sacs, however, and cannot engage in anal respiration.

Many soft-shells are quite aggressive (*ferox*, the Latin name for the Florida soft-shell, means "wild" or "savage"), so their long necks also enable them to easily reach around and bite anyone attempting to capture or pick them up.

An efficient way to capture soft-shells buried in the mud Carr (citing the master's thesis of Lewis Marchand) reports, is to "thrust the hand into the mud until the carapace is felt, then to slide the hand forward until the anterior margin of the shell is reached. The fingers are then gently slipped around the animal's neck, and when a secure hold has been obtained, all possible pressure is applied and the turtle is pulled up through the water and thrown into the boat...a vigorous choking grip may be necessary to discourage attempts at biting." Definitely a procedure best left to the dedicated turtle enthusiast!

Most species (sixteen) of soft-shell turtle belong to the genus *Trionyx* and are found, among other places, in the United States, Mexico, most of Africa, Syria, Iraq, India, Burma, China, Japan, Taiwan, and Vietnam. In countries other than the United States, the habits of the soft-shell turtle frequently are little known, because the principal interest people have in it is as a source of food.

In North America, the most common soft-shell turtle is the spiny soft-shell (*Trionyx spinifer*), which gets its name from tiny, conical projections along the anterior (front) margins of the carapace. There are currently six recognized subspecies of the spiny soft-shell. In the United States, it lives throughout most of the eastern, central, and southern states; its range extends west to the

© Dr. E.R. Degginger

Rocky Mountains, across Texas and into the Southwest. In Canada, it is found in southern Quebec and Ontario; in Mexico for 100 to 200 miles (160 to 320 kilometers) south of the Mexico-United States border.

The spiny soft-shell is a medium- to large-sized soft-shell turtle whose leathery shell has a sandpaper-like surface. Females grow to 20 inches (50 centimeters); males to 10 inches (25 centimeters). The color of its shell ranges from olive to tan, with a pattern of

dark ocelli (circular markings, often with dark centers) or blotches and one or two dark lines around the margin; the plastron is an unmarked white or yellow; its head has two light stripes with dark borders on the side.

Spiny soft-shells live in a variety of watery habitats with soft bottoms and aquatic vegetation: marshes, creeks, ponds, bayous, rivers, and lakes. They spend most of their time foraging for food at the surface or, as mentioned above, buried in the bottom with only their heads and necks protruding. Spiny soft-shells are primarily carnivorous, eating crayfish, insects, earthworms, fish, tadpoles, and frogs. Sometimes they swim along the bottom, feeding in what appears to be a random fashion; at other times, they deliberately pursue prey or lie in ambush waiting for it.

As do many other aquatic turtles in the Western Hemisphere, soft-shells in northern

The eastern spiny soft-shell *(Trionyx spiniferus spiniferus)*, a subspecies that lives east of the Mississippi River and as far south as northern Alabama.

areas hibernate underwater from November to April; in southern areas, they are active all year. Nests are usually built in June or July; clutches average twenty hard-shelled, brittle eggs slightly larger than 1 inch (2.5 centimeters) in diameter. Raccoons and skunks raid their nests, and fish, other turtles, snakes, birds, and mammals eat the young. The only threat to adults are alligators and human beings. There is evidence that the spiny soft-shell can live to be sixty years of age or older.

Five species of soft-shell turtles are found in Africa, most of them quite large. The Nubian soft-shell, Aubrey's soft-shell, and the Zambesi soft-shell may all reach a carapace length of more than 2 feet (60 centimeters); the Nile soft-shell may grow to a carapace length of more than 3 feet (90 centimeters). Pritchard reported a population of Nile soft-shell turtles living in six to fifteen fathoms (eleven to twenty-eight meters) of sea water off the coast of Turkey. The animals were numerous enough to pester fishermen all along the coast, and were considered so vicious that fishermen did not like to bring them into their boats.

Six species of soft-shells live in or near India. One, the Indian flap-shelled turtle, is small (males: 6 inches [15 centimeters]; females: 11 inches [28 centimeters]) and is distinguished by its domed carapace and (in some subspecies) the yellow spots on its shell. Another species, the Indian soft-shell, is known for its great size (around 5 feet [1.5 meters] long), flipperlike feet, and the absence of a clear distinction between the anterior carapace and the neck. The shell seems to form itself into a funnel at the neck. From the end of the funnel, a small, narrow head with eyes very near the snout, emerges. Large specimens of the Indian soft-shell have been reported to attack and wreck small boats.

One species living in Bangladesh, *Trionyx nigricans,* apparently no longer exists in the wild. For more than 100 years, a semicaptive colony of these large turtles has been kept as a part of a religious shrine. Some are quite large (carapaces of about 3 feet [1 meter]) and tame, coming to feed when called.

Other species live in Burma and Malaya; the Chinese soft-shell (*Trionyx sinensis*) is found in China, Taiwan, Korea, Japan, and has even been introduced in Hawaii.

Opposite page: Painted turtles (Chrysemys picta) are found in the eastern seaboard of North America, from Nova Scotia south to northern Georgia. *Overleaf:* The yellow-bellied turtle (Chrysemys scripta) has a thick, deep, strongly sculpted carapace.

SEMIAQUATIC TURTLES

The Emydidae is the largest family of living turtles, comprising some thirty genera and eighty-five species. Emydid turtles are largely freshwater and semiterrestrial turtles: Many divide their time between land and water and spend a good deal of time basking; some, which resemble tortoises, spend most of their time on land.

Emydid turtles range in size from the 4-inch (10-centimeter) bog turtle, which lives in the United States, to the batagur turtle of Southeast Asia, which grows to a carapace length of 2 feet (60 centimeters) and may weigh 60 pounds (22 kilograms).

Most emydid turtles live in the northern hemisphere, though a few Asian species live south of the equator. Emydid turtles are found in the greatest abundance and variety in eastern North America and Southeast Asia. They also live in Central and South America and India; only a handful of species are found in Europe, Africa, and the Middle East. No emydid turtles live in Australia.

In North America, there are three distinct groups of emydid turtles: basking turtles, map turtles, and terrapins, most of which have short necks, broad jaw surfaces, and a preference for running water (rivers and streams), although many basking turtles prefer still water; pond and box turtles, which have short necks, narrow jaw surfaces, and a tendency to live on land; and chicken and Blanding's turtles, which have long necks, narrow jaw surfaces, and a preference for relatively still waters.

BASKING TURTLES, MAP TURTLES, AND TERRAPINS

Basking Turtles

Basking turtles include about fourteen species and thirty-three subspecies which are found in the southeastern and south-central United States, including Illinois, Indiana, Missouri, Kentucky, Tennessee, North and South Carolina, Georgia, Alabama, Mississippi, Arkansas, Louisiana, Oklahoma, and

Above: A closeup of a red-eared slider *(Trachemys scripta elegans). Right:* Note the red "ear patch" and highly decorative shell.

© A.B. Sheldon

chemyd turtles are known as sliders; pseude-myds as cooters and red bellies; and chrysemyds as painted turtles.

Most people would immediately recognize the genus because it includes the most widely kept pet turtle in the world, *Trachemys scripta elegans,* commonly known as the red-eared slider (because of the red patch behind its ear and its habit, in the wild, of sliding off the logs on which it frequently basks, into the water when it senses danger approaching).

Baby red-eared sliders were once raised and sold by the millions in "turtle farms" in the United States and Europe. Then, in the 1970s, salmonella infections in humans were traced to pet *Trachemys scripta elegans,* and the sale of baby sliders was prohibited. This was a blessing for the turtles, because they are quite delicate as juveniles and, because of neglect and inadvertent mistreatment, often lived no more than two months. Adult red-ears, which are much hardier animals, are still commonly available in pet stores.

Basking turtles are medium- to large-sized turtles (8 to 16 inches [20 to 41 centimeters]) that spend much of their time on logs, rocks, or banks adjacent to water, sometimes gathering in large groups. They prefer aquatic habitats with soft bottoms and abundant vegetation. Males are usually smaller than females (sometimes half the size) and are easily identified by the extremely long claws found on their front feet, which are used to stroke the female's face in courtship.

Basking turtles have oval, moderately domed carapaces, sometimes with elaborate geometrical patterns. Often the marginal plates are a bright color, such as red or yellow, that contrasts with the green, brown, or black carapace. The skin of the head and feet is generally green, olive, or black, with contrasting, longitudinal yellow stripes. Behind the eye is a red, orange, or yellow horizontal line or spot. The skin of the head is relatively smooth, while the feet are somewhat more scaly. The plastron is usually bright yellow or red, sometimes with intricate configurations in a contrasting color. As they age, the carapaces of both males and females frequently become dark, losing all color patterning.

Depending on their age, basking turtles

Texas. In addition, the genus extends into Mexico, Central America, the northwest corner of South America, southern Brazil, and northern Argentina. It is found also on the Cayman Islands, Cuba, Jamaica, Puerto Rico, and the Bahamas.

Until recently (the mid-1980s), basking turtles typically were grouped into two genera, *Pseudemys* and *Chrysemys,* the latter consisting of a single species, *Chrysemys picta,* the painted turtle. Now, a third designation, *Trachemys,* is used. Popularly, tra-

© A.B. Sheldon

A juvenile Suwanee cooter *(Pseudemys concinna suwannensis)* basks in the sun.

prefer different sorts of food. When young, they often choose meat, but as they grow older they eat progressively larger amounts of vegetable matter. Adults are omnivorous and will eat any food available.

Typically, basking turtles are mild-mannered, preferring to retreat or escape when threatened. They are diurnal: sleeping at night, basking on logs or the water's surface from midmorning to midafternoon, and feeding mostly in the early morning and late afternoon. In late fall, basking turtles hibernate, usually underwater or in muskrat burrows, but if there is a winter warm spell, they may become temporarily active. Basking turtles normally remain in one place, near good basking and feeding sites. They

typically nest in June or July, laying about fifteen oval eggs usually more than once per season. Basking turtles are generally hardy and may live thirty years or more.

Their nests are raided by opossums, skunks, bears, and raccoons. Snakes, large wading birds, large fish, carnivorous turtles, and the above-mentioned mammals eat juveniles. Alligators, mammals, and humans eat adults, and humans destroy many more, both willfully (shooting them, running over them in cars) and through ignorance (keeping them as pets but not bothering to find out their needs). Ernst and Barbour's comment about the red-eared slider applies to the genus as a whole: "It is a marvel that the species survives."

Top: A male Texas slider *(Pseudemys texana):* Note the long claws characteristic of males.

Middle left: The hieroglyphic slider *(Pseudemys concinna hieroglyphica),* a large emydid living in the south-central states of the United States.

Middle right: The Alabama red-bellied turtle *(Pseudemys rubriventris alabamensis)* is a rare turtle found only in the vicinity of Mobile Bay, Alabama.

Bottom: The Missouri slider *(Pseudemys floridana hoyi)* lives in the central United States.

© Dr. E.R. Degginger

Map Turtles

Map turtles (genus *Graptemys*) consist of ten species of medium-sized, highly aquatic turtles that live, for the most part, in river systems of the eastern and central United States. Five of the ten species, however, live in southern Mississippi and Alabama, and two are found only in Texas.

Map turtles get their name from the intricate patterns of yellow or cream-colored lines (resembling the lines of topographical maps) on their green or brown carapaces. Three well-known species are the common map turtle (*Graptemys geographica*), the black-knobbed sawback (*Graptemys nigrinoda*), and the false map turtle (*Graptemys pseudogeographica*).

Map turtles have striped and patterned heads and limbs, similar to painted turtles and sliders. On many species, the carapace has a ridge of pointed projections, which accounts for the nickname "sawback."

There are extreme differences, both physical and behavioral, between the sexes among map turtles. In several species females may be more than twice as large as males. For instance, the largest Barbour's map turtle (*Graptemys barbouri*) on record, a female, had a carapace length of almost 13 inches (33 centimeters); males are not known to exceed 5 inches (13 centimeters). (Females of other species range in size from 5 to 11 inches [13 to 27 centimeters], males from 4 to 6 inches [10 to 15 centimeters].)

Females also develop very large heads (the above specimen had a head 3 inches [8 centimeters] wide) with broad jaw surfaces, which they use to crush the shellfish that form a significant part of their diets. Alternately, males have small, narrow heads and jaw surfaces and are likely to eat softer animals, such as insects and worms. Both sexes eat some vegetable matter as well.

Further, males tend to be found basking in the vicinity of partially submerged tree branches and logs near the banks of rivers; females inhabit the muddy areas of river bottoms. In general, map turtles are shy and wary of danger. They do not do well in captivity.

The Alabama map turtle (*Graptemys pulchre*) is characterized by a black line along the vertebral ridge.

© Dr. E.R. Degginger

© Dr. E.R. Degginger

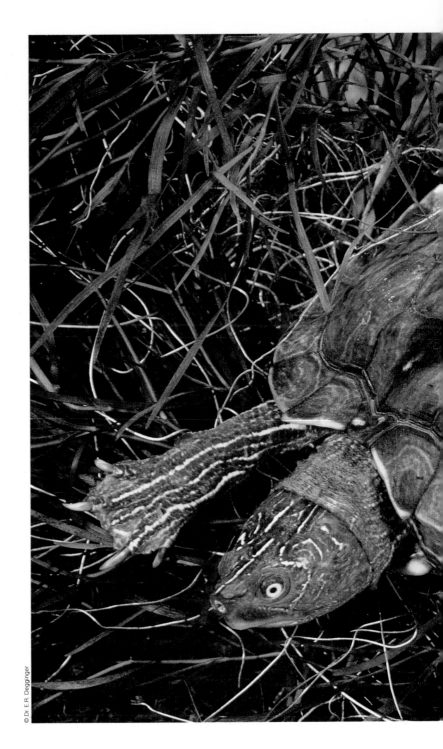

© Dr. E.R. Degginger

Map turtles are found throughout the eastern and southern United States. Many species have raised or pointed median projections, which gives rise to the common name "sawback." *Above, top:* The black-knobbed sawback *(Graptemys nigrinoda pelticola)* is found mostly in Alabama and Mississippi. *Above, bottom:* The ringed sawback lives only in the Pearl River of southern Mississippi and adjacent Louisiana. *Above, right:* The Mississippi map turtle *(Graptemys kohni)* can always be identified by its distinctive white iris and the light crescent behind each eye. *Right:* The Sabine map turtle *(Graptemys pseudogeographica sabinensis)* is a subspecies of the false map turtle. It is found in the Sabine River, which separates Louisiana from Texas. *Far right:* The Barbour's map turtle *(Graptemys barbouri)* exhibits extreme sexual dimorphism: Females are sometimes more than twice as large as males.

© Dr. E.R. Degginger

© Dr. E.R. Degginger

Above: Ornate diamondback terrapins *(Malaclemys macrospilota)* are identified by the orange-yellow centers of the carapacial scutes. Along with green turtle soup, the use of diamondback terrapins as a luxury food item is perhaps the most celebrated example of turtle cuisine. From the late 1800s until about 1920, terrapin meat was a much-sought-after commodity, and many terrapins were raised commercially.

Terrapins

Closely related to map turtles, diamondback terrapins (genus *Malaclemys*) consist of one species (*Malaclemys terrapin*) and seven subspecies, found exclusively in coastal waters and brackish marshes, estuaries, and lagoons from Massachusetts all the way to the Gulf coast of southeast Texas.

Diamondback terrapins are medium-sized turtles (5 to 10 inches [13 to 25 centimeters] long); the head is thick and blunt, and the head and legs are covered with spots instead of stripes. Most species have strongly inscribed, concentric rings on the carapace plates; these are raised in the center, accounting for the name "diamondback." They have large, webbed rear feet.

As with map turtles, female diamondbacks are nearly twice as large as males and have larger heads. Diamondbacks are primarily carnivorous, and some of their food is obtained by scavenging. They hibernate in winter, though they may emerge for warm periods. They are most active during the day and sleep buried in the mud at night.

Diamondbacks are perhaps best known for their popularity as a gourmet food item during the late nineteenth century and in the 1920s. In fact, large "farms" were established (notably at Beaufort, North Carolina) to raise them; ironically, this measure undoubtedly saved some populations from decimation and perhaps extinction.

Archie Carr characterized the diamondback's popularity as a delicacy as largely a fad "as synthetic as the latest Paris fashion. I don't mean to say that diamondbacks aren't good eating," he said. "I merely suggest that the difference between a seven-dollar diamondback and a forty-cent soft-shell of the same weight is to a considerable degree a difference in the state of mind of the consumer."

© A.B. Sheldon

© David M. Dennis/Tom Stack & Associates

Above: The head of a northern diamondback terrapin, found from Cape Cod south to Cape Hatteras, North Carolina. *Left:* This variety of Caspian turtle, *Mauremys caspica caspica,* lives in western Iran, Iraq, and parts of Turkey.

POND AND BOX TURTLES

Pond Turtles

In North America, there are four species of pond turtles (genus *Clemmys*), popularly known as the spotted turtle, the wood turtle, the bog turtle (or Muhlenberg's turtle), and the Western pond turtle. The first three, which are found only in the northeastern United States and adjoining parts of Canada, are equally aquatic and terrestrial, while the Western pond turtle (which lives on the West Coast of North America, from the state of Washington south into Baja California) rarely leaves the water except to bask.

Generally, pond turtles are medium-sized (5 to 9 inches [13 to 23 centimeters] in carapace length). The bog turtle, however, is an exception; at slightly more than 4 inches (10 centimeters), it may be the smallest species of turtle in the world. All species are omnivorous, eating worms, snails, insects, crayfish, carrion, as well as fruits and grasses. The Western pond turtle is the most carnivorous.

Male and female pond turtles are about the same size, and with the exception that males usually have a concave plastron, the sexes are not dramatically different in appearance. Females lay from three to twelve eggs in shallow nests, which they frequently take great care to camouflage.

The spotted turtle (*Clemmys guttata*) has a smooth, bluish black carapace with yellow spots. Juveniles have very few spots, and more appear as the animal gets older. The spots may fade on very old specimens. The skin is gray to black and is occasionally spotted, too.

Spotted turtles are small (4 to 5 inches [10 to 13 centimeters]), mild-mannered, and shy; they burrow in the mud when disturbed in the water and retreat into their shells when threatened on land. Compared with most emydid turtles, they prefer cold temperatures, though they hibernate underwater in the coldest parts of winter. Spotted turtles have recorded lifespans of more than forty years.

Above, top: The spotted turtle *(Clemmys guttata)* and wood turtle *(Clemmys insculpta [above, bottom])* are emydids that live in the eastern and northeastern United States. The latter is hardy and intelligent, making it a suitable pet, though it is protected over much of its range.

© A.B. Sheldon

The wood turtle (*Clemmys insculpta*) is larger than the spotted turtle, averaging about 7 inches (18 centimeters) in length. Striking in appearance, it has a rough, keeled shell that flares at the edges; a flat, frequently jet-black head; orange limbs and throat; and a long tail. As the name implies, wood turtles are mainly terrestrial, frequenting bodies of water only at times of mating or hibernation.

Wood turtles are most active during the day, when they wander about in woods and meadows. Their range appears to be limited; individuals who have been captured and released frequently are recaptured, even years later, very close to where they were originally found. Wood turtles are accomplished climbers—they have been seen ascending chainlink fences. The oldest wood turtle on record lived fifty-eight years.

Many authorities comment on the superior intelligence of the wood turtle. Archie Carr cites some experiments with mazes in which it was "decided that its ability to learn new routes was about equal to that of a rat, which, though it has an uncomplimentary ring, is really pretty good for a turtle; and anyway, in a personality contest a wood turtle would win from a rat in a walk."

Because of its intelligence and genial, extroverted nature, wood turtles are prized as pets by many turtle collectors. Carr kept one in the house for eighteen months: "She slept in a closet and showed up at the breakfast table every morning where she made for my wife's chair, craned her neck expectantly, and often stood on three legs with one foot lifted and poised like a pointer dog that smells birds."

Bog turtles (*Clemmys muhlenbergi*) have,

The bog turtle *(Clemmys muhlenbergi)*, or Muhlenberg's turtle, is perhaps the smallest species of turtle in the world, rarely exceeding 4 inches (10 cm) in length.

©A.B. Sheldon

Spotted turtles *(Clemmys guttata)* are fairly small animals, rarely exceeding 5 inches (13 cm) in carapace length.

according to Pritchard, "perhaps the most rigid habitat preferences of any North American freshwater turtle. It is usually found in sphagnum bogs, in situations where it can walk about in very shallow water."

The bog turtle is of interest for its small size and discontinuous range (it is found in parts of New York, New Jersey, Massachusetts, Connecticut, Pennsylvania, and Maryland). Human beings are rapidly encroaching on the bog turtle's territory, and it is a threatened species.

The range of pond turtles in North America extends only as far west as Wisconsin, and then, oddly, it picks up again on the West Coast with the Pacific pond turtle (*Clemmys marmorata*). Medium-sized (about 6 inches [15 centimeters]) and olive to black in color, it is thoroughly aquatic except when basking or digging a nest. Shy and wary, it plunges into the water at the least disturbance.

Box Turtles

Four species of box turtles (genus *Terrapene*) inhabit North America: Two are abundant and widespread in the United States, while smaller populations of all four species are found in Mexico.

Box turtles, which are largely terrestrial, are medium-sized turtles (6 to 8 inches [15 to 20 centimeters] long) with several distinctive physical features: a colorful, ornate, domed shell that is longer than it is wide; a plastral hinge that allows them to withdraw completely into their shells; and large rear feet, which are neither webbed (and therefore unsuited for swimming) nor elephantine (like the feet of the tortoises that box turtles resemble). Additionally, the upper jaws of box turtles have a slight hook at the tip, and the rear feet have prominent claws. Male box turtles have bright red eyes; the female's are light brown.

Box turtles are strictly diurnal; after dark, they burrow or find some place to conceal themselves for the night. Their home range is limited (a radius of several hundred yards is typical). Box turtles are omnivorous, eating fruit, carrion, vegetation, insects, small vertebrates, and worms.

Nesting takes place from May through July; clutch sizes range from two to eight eggs. Nests are destroyed by skunks, foxes, raccoons, and crows. Snakes, crows, coyotes, foxes, dogs, and skunks eat juveniles. Man is the greatest destroyer of adult box turtles—thousands are crushed on the highway every year. Because it is hardy, even-tempered, adaptable, and long-lived, the box turtle, like the wood turtle, is a favored pet among turtle fanciers.

The eastern box turtle (*Terrapene carolina*) is found primarily in the open woods of almost every state south of the Great Lakes and east of the Mississippi River, plus Kansas, Missouri, Oklahoma, Arkansas, Louisiana, eastern Texas, and the Mexican states of Campeche, Quintana Roo, San Luis Potosi, Tamaulipas, Veracruz, and Yucatan.

Usually, the eastern box turtle has a brown or black carapace decorated with red or yellow stripes, dots, or smudges, often in a pattern that looks like it might have been painted by a small child.

The western (or "ornate") box turtle (*Terrapene ornata*) inhabits the treeless plains, prairies, and rolling country covered with grass and scattered low brush in the southwestern, central, and south-central United States and western Mexico. It is smaller than the eastern box turtle, the maximum length being about 6 inches (15 centimeters). The decorative pattern on the western box turtle's shell is somewhat different, too: It has a dark brown or black carapace with yellow lines radiating outward from the center of each scute.

CHICKEN AND BLANDING'S TURTLES

The remaining emydid turtles in the United States consist of two genera of one species each, Blanding's turtle (*Emydoidea blandingi*) and the chicken turtle (*Deirochelys reticularia*). Both are medium-sized turtles (maximum size: about 10 inches [25 centimeters]) with long necks and narrow jaw surfaces; both prefer still waters, such as ponds, swamps, and drainage ditches.

The Blanding's turtle lives in the north-central United States—near the Great Lakes and slightly to the west—and just north, in southern Canada. It has a smooth, dark carapace covered with yellow speckles and resembles a European pond turtle, to which it was once thought to be closely related. It has several other distinguishing features; prominent eyes, a long neck, a plastral hinge, and a yellow throat and lower jaw. Blanding's turtles, which are completely aquatic except for when they bask, are omnivorous but show a preference for crayfish.

The chicken turtle (named for the taste of its flesh) is found in the southern and south-central United States. It has a medium-brown, slightly sculpted shell, a striped neck two-thirds the length of its carapace, and distinctive vertical stripes on its thighs. It is omnivorous but prefers small invertebrates. Unlike Blanding's turtle, the chicken turtle spends a good deal of time wandering on land.

OTHER NEW WORLD EMYDIDS

One other genus of emydid turtles is found in the Western Hemisphere. Known as *Rhinoclemys,* it consists of nine species of terrestrial and semiterrestrial turtles that range from southern Sonora, in western Mexico, southward through Central America, and into Ecuador and northern Brazil in South America.

These turtles resemble box turtles, but they are larger and lack a plastral hinge. All have been fully described by herpetologists,

The Florida box turtle *(Terrapene carolina bauri)* resides in southern Georgia and throughout Florida.

© A.B. Sheldon

Above: Blanding's turtle (*Emydoidea blandingi*), a medium-sized, carnivorous North American emydid. *Right:* A closeup of a box turtle. Interestingly, box turtle meat is frequently poisonous to humans because of residue from poisonous fungi that make up part of the turtle's diet.

© Steven Morello

but little is known about the habits of many members of this genus, so only the most significant and/or unusual will be included here.

One widespread species is known popularly as the Mexican red turtle or Mexican wood turtle (*Rhinoclemys pulcherrima*), which lives in Mexico and Central America and is distinguished by thin red and black wormlike lines on its face, limbs, and tail. This is an omnivorous, fundamentally terrestrial turtle that grows to a typical carapace length of about 6 inches (15 centimeters). The largest and most aquatic member of the genus is *Rhinoclemys funera,* which is found in eastern Central America. It has a black carapace and grows to a maximum length of 13 inches (33 centimeters).

South American varieties of *Rhinoclemys* are unusual in that females usually lay a single, large egg (3 inches by 1½ inches [8 centimeters by 4 centimeters]) that is sometimes nearly half the length of the turtle itself. In tropical climates, several eggs can be laid each year, and the larger hatchlings have a better chance to survive.

EUROPEAN EMYDIDS

The principal difference between the way emydid turtles are distributed in the Americas and in Europe is that in the Americas there are relatively few genera but many species, while in Europe, there are many genera but few species; in fact, many genera consist of but a single species.

Only three species of emydid turtles live in areas surrounding the Mediterranean Sea. One of the best known is the European pond turtle (*Emys orbicularis*), which resembles Blanding's turtle, having a black carapace with light yellow speckles. It is found in Spain, central France, northern Italy, southern Germany, Poland, northern Turkey and Iran, northern Morocco, Algeria, and Tunisia. This small (5 to 6 inch [13 to 15 centimeters]), carnivorous turtle has been popular as a pet among British turtle fanciers, though the weather in England is too cold for pond turtles that live outdoors to breed.

Another Mediterranean emydid is the Spanish turtle (*Mauremys leprosa*), which lives in Spain, Portugal, Morocco, Algeria,

Libya, and Tunisia. An aquatic, carnivorous species, the Spanish turtle often lives in filthy mudholes and becomes infested with parasites and covered with algae; hence, its Latin name.

A close relative, the Caspian turtle (*Mauremys caspica*), lives in the Middle East (Iran, Iraq, Turkey, Syria, and Israel) as well as parts of Greece, Crete, and Yugoslavia. The male Caspian turtle is reputed to be extremely violent toward the female during mating, biting her neck with such viciousness that the wounds often prove fatal. Two relatives of the Caspian turtle, *Mauremys mutica* and *Mauremys japonica,* live in China and southern Japan, respectively.

ASIAN EMYDIDS

The rest of the world's emydid turtles, some thirty-plus genera, live in Asia—principally in India, Bangladesh, China, Taiwan, and mainland Southeast Asia (including Burma, Thailand, Vietnam, and Malaysia).

Little is known of the behavior of many of these asiatic turtles, so again only the most significant and unusual are described here.

The Brahminy river turtle (*Hardella thurji*) lives in the Ganges, Brahmaputra, and Indus river systems in India. A large turtle (females grow to 21 inches [53 centi-

The serrated turtle, a large east African sideneck, often reaches a length of more than 15 inches (38 cm) and a weight of more than 20 pounds (8 kg).

meters]), it is an important food source, and great numbers are sold in Calcutta. The size differences between males and females are greater in this species than in any other known species; males grow to a reported maximum length of just 7 inches (18 centimeters). The Brahminy river turtle is herbivorous and is reported to have a gentle disposition. Its carapace is dark brown or black.

Another large aquatic species is the common batagur or tuntong (*Batagur baska*), found in the rivers of Sumatra, Thailand, Burma, and the Malay Peninsula. It grows to a length of about 2 feet (61 centimeters), and females lay clutches of ten to thirty eggs, 3 inches (8 centimeters) long, which are collected by the humans in the countries where they are found.

The turtle gets the second of its popular names from the drumming sound a nesting female makes—"tun tonk"—when she drops herself on the sand to compact her nest after laying the eggs and covering them. Sometimes natives can hear hundreds of batagurs nesting simultaneously.

The biuku turtle (*Callagur borneoensis*), found in Borneo, Sumatra, and the Malay Peninsula, may be the largest of all emydid turtles, reaching a carapace length of 30 inches (76 centimeters). Its distinctive features are a covering of skin (instead of scales) on top of its head and a gray-brown carapace with three black, longitudinal bands.

The spiny turtle (*Heosemys spinosa*), an emydid from Southeast Asia that grows to 8 or 9 inches (20 or 23 centimeters) long, looks like a cogwheel; it has a raised, spiny keel and marginals (scutes around the edge of the carapace).

Three of the five Asiatic box turtles (genus *Cuora*), like their American counterparts (*Terrapene*), have well-developed plastral hinges, which allow them to shut their soft parts completely within the protective surrounding of their shells. One of the more abundant species is the Malayan box turtle (*Cuora amboinensis*), an herbivorous species that is mostly aquatic, inhabiting ponds, marshes, and flooded rice paddies.

A turtle common to southern China that has also been introduced to other parts of the world (including the United States) is Reeves' turtle (*Chinemys reevesi*). It grows to slightly more than 12 inches (31 centimeters) in length and has brown carapace scutes edged in yellow or white. An omnivorous turtle that is hardy in captivity, Reeves' turtle is popular as a pet.

Reeves' turtle *(Chinemys reevesi)*, an Asian emydid, possesses a hardy constitution, and as such is popular as a pet.

TORTOISES

Next to emydid turtles, tortoises (family Testudinidae) make up the largest category of the world's chelonians: There are ten genera and about thirty-nine species worldwide, the greatest diversity of which are found in Africa.

Tortoises are the only turtles—except for a few emydids—completely adapted for life on land. They differ from other types of turtles in several ways: they have hard, horny shells with distinct, well-defined growth rings (annuli) on each lamina; front feet that are slightly flattened from front to back, with thick scales on the front; stumplike, elephantine rear legs; a mostly herbivorous diet; and an almost exclusively terrestrial habitat. Tortoises are generally considered to have evolved from emydid turtles.

It is not possible to talk about tortoises without bringing human beings into the discussion in a significant way, because, begin-ning about 400 years ago, mankind has had a crucial, devastating, and irreversible influence on the very existence of many species of tortoises—millions were slaughtered, and nearly a dozen species (all of the genus *Geochelone*) are now considered "recently extinct" or "almost extinct." In some ways, the manner in which people treated tortoises in the seventeenth and eighteenth centuries parallels the way many species of sea turtles have been treated in modern times.

The largest and most widely distributed genus of tortoises is *Geochelone*; sixteen species are found throughout Africa, Southeast Asia, Madagascar, Celebes (an island in Indonesia), Aldabra (an island in the Indian Ocean), and the Galapagos Islands (east of Ecuador). All larger tortoises belong to this genus; the most famous are the gigantic species inhabiting the Galapagos Islands and those, similar in appearance but descended from different ancestors, now living almost half a world away on the island of Aldabra.

A Galapagos tortoise (*Geochelone elephantopus*) may reach a carapace length of 4 feet (1.2 m) and a weight of 500 pounds (187 kg). Its legs are extremely strong and are capable of bearing a man's weight on its back.

GALAPAGOS TORTOISES

The Galapagos Islands lie about 600 miles (960 kilometers) east of Ecuador, on the equator. Comprised of a group of about twenty volcanic islands, the Galapagos archipelago was discovered by Spanish sailors in 1535. Giant tortoises (*Geochelone elephantopus*) lived on eleven of these islands in incredibly abundant numbers. In many places, it has been written, the islands were so densely populated with tortoises that a person could walk on their backs for long distances without ever setting foot on the ground beneath them.

Originally, there were about fourteen different subspecies of tortoises living on the Galapagos, separated from each other by the ocean or impassable stretches of fresh lava. Galapagos tortoises reach a maximum carapace length of nearly 4 feet (1.2 meters) and may weigh 500 pounds (187 kilograms) or more. The shape of the carapace varies depending on the subspecies—some are domed, some are flatter, some are distinctly "saddlebacked" (elevated above the neck). The color of the carapace is dark brown, dark green, or black. Head and neck size also vary according to subspecies, though most have long necks, which allows them to reach plants that grow several feet off the ground, such as certain varieties of cactus. With their large, powerful legs, the giant tortoises are able to scramble over rocky ground.

Male Galapagos tortoises are much larger than females; their size advantage helps them in courtship rituals, which are abbreviated and direct: Males simply overpower females, battering them with the front of their shells and immobilizing them with their weight. Females nest throughout the year, choosing a place that receives direct sunlight. A clutch of ten eggs is typical. Both males and females mature slowly, taking about twenty to twenty-five years.

Galapagos tortoises spend much of their time wallowing in the mud near water holes and swamps. Depending on the ambient temperature, they may partially submerge themselves in ponds. At night, many burrow in soft ground or vegetation. In dry weather, Galapagos tortoises migrate to the moist highlands, moving back to the lowlands during periods of rainy weather. They will eat al-

© Ann Reilly/Photo/Nats

most any green vegetation they can find.

These tortoises lived relatively undisturbed until the nineteenth century, when hunters in search of seals and whales landed on the islands. Galapagos tortoises became a readily available source of meat for these men. At first, whalers simply brought large numbers of the mild-mannered tortoises on board ship where, left virtually unattended

and uncared for, they were killed as needed.

Later, when whales became scarce, the hunters discovered that oil could be obtained from the fat and eggs of tortoises. According to whalers' logs, some 200,000 were slaughtered, often wastefully, within a thirty-year period, and it has been estimated that more than 10 million have been killed since the discovery of the Galapagos Islands nearly 500 years ago. Tortoises also perished as a result of the cultivation of the land and consequent destruction of their habitats, and through the introduction of feral mammals such as dogs, goats, pigs, and rats, which compete for food, destroy nests, and kill juveniles.

In this century, conservation and breeding programs have been undertaken, and al-

Over the centuries, hundreds of thousands, possibly millions, of Galapagos tortoises have been slaughtered by human beings.

though several subspecies have become extinct or endangered, there are perhaps 10,000 tortoises remaining in the Galapagos today, and they are not considered critically endangered.

In 1964, two significant steps were taken to ensure the tortoises' well-being: The Darwin Memorial Research Station was founded on one of the islands, and the archipelago was established as a national park of Ecuador, further protecting the tortoise. One of the most important tasks that has been undertaken to preserve the tortoise is the destruction of the wild animals with which they cannot successfully compete.

Less well known but equally tragic was the fate of the subspecies of giant tortoises living on islands in the Indian Ocean, which were very similar in appearance to those on the Galapagos Islands.

In the sixteenth century, travellers rounding the Cape of Good Hope heading toward India discovered a number of islands inhabited by unusual animals. In 1598, the first Dutch sailors reached Mauritius, a small island east of Madagascar. Here they found large, trusting, flightless birds and giant tortoises, both of whom they slaughtered in huge numbers.

It only took a few years for the birds—dodos—to become extinct, and by the mid-1700s, the number of tortoises on Mauritius had been drastically reduced. They were found to be living on nearby smaller islands, and were imported to Mauritius to be sold to passing naval, merchant, or pirate ships. Gradually, island by island, the giant tortoises on Diego Rodriguez, Reunion, Mauritius, Farquhar, and the Seychelles Archipelago were almost completely exterminated.

By the end of the nineteenth century the only significant numbers of giant tortoises were those living on the island of Aldabra. They survived only because the island is off the direct sea route to India.

To prevent the destruction of all the giants, a number of famous British naturalists —Charles Darwin among them—initiated protective measures, mainly exportation and captive breeding. Tortoises from Aldabra were taken to Mauritius, and breeding farms were established. Today, about 100,000 tortoises live in the wild and on Aldabra; tortoises are also found in lesser numbers on Mauritius and Zanzibar.

Giant tortoises have the potential to live very long lives. Several are on record as having lived more than 100 years. Perhaps the oldest, known as "Marion's tortoise" of Mauritius, lived for 152 years before an accident ended its life in 1918.

Because of their great size and, therefore, their economic value, the giant tortoises of the Galapagos and the islands off Madagascar are unique in the extent to which they have been exploited by human beings.

Right: Steps have been taken by the government of Ecuador and private organizations to preserve the Galapagos tortoise. *Opposite page:* Originally, there were fourteen distinct populations of giant tortoises on the Galapagos Islands before man began to kill them in large numbers in the nineteenth century.

The leopard tortoise, a large African species with distinctive markings and a domed carapace.

OTHER TORTOISES FROM AFRICA AND MADAGASCAR

Other significant African tortoises of the genus *Geochelone* include the spurred tortoise and the leopard tortoise. The spurred tortoise (*Geochelone sulcata*), found across the broadest section of north-central Africa, is the largest mainland tortoise, growing to more than 30 inches (76 centimeters) and 200 pounds (75 kilograms). Males are much bigger than females.

The carapace of the spurred tortoise is a uniform yellow or bone color; the laminae and growth rings are generally well defined. The spurred tortoise is named for two or three strong spines, or spurs, on each side of its tail. Because it lives in arid desert regions, the spurred tortoise may have to go without water for years at a time. A thick, highly impermeable skin, plus its habit of digging deep burrows in hot weather, prevent moisture loss.

The leopard tortoise (*Geochelone pardalis*) is smaller (2 feet [60 centimeters] long, 70 pounds [26 kilograms]) than the spurred tortoise; its range extends over the plains of most of central and southern Africa, where there is more vegetation available than in the range of the spurred tortoise. A hardy species, the leopard tortoise makes a good pet. Not surprisingly, it is named for its domed, decorative carapace—black spots and blotches on a yellow background.

Each of the laminae of the radiated tortoise of Madagascar (*Geochelone radiata*) are slightly conical, with a black-on-yellow star pattern radiating from the center. Males and females grow to about 15 inches (38 centimeters) and a weight of 28 pounds (10 kilograms). Radiated tortoises are protected by law and venerated by natives, who will not harm them. Unfortunately, many Chinese in Madagascar will pay a high price for the turtle, because they consider its flesh to be an aphrodisiac. The starred tortoise of India (*Geochelone elegans*) is very similar to the radiated tortoise, but smaller (females grow to 10 inches [25 centimeters]; males to 6 inches [15 centimeters]).

One of the most famous and long-lived of all turtles was a radiated tortoise, "Tui Malila," reputedly presented to the Queen of Tonga by Captain Cook in 1773 or 1777. It lived until May 19, 1966—and survived at least one forest fire as well as a severe kick by a horse. At the end of its life, it was completely blind and had to be fed by hand.

One of the most interesting African tortoises is the pancake tortoise (*Malacochersus tornieri*), which lives in Kenya and Tanzania. Unlike other tortoises, which have hard, domed shells, the pancake tortoise has a flat, soft shell. Pancake tortoises reach a length of about 6 inches (15 centimeters); the carapace is usually pale brown with dark brown or black borders to the laminae. The pancake tortoise eats vegetation; females lay a single egg.

Pancake tortoises are capable of climbing rocks and can typically be found under them. When molested, instead of withdrawing into its shell, the pancake tortoise runs and wedges itself into a rocky crevice. There, it inflates its lungs, rendering itself nearly immovable.

The hinge-back tortoise (*Kinixys erosa*), which lives across most of central Africa just north of the equator, is unique in that it is the only tortoise with a hinged carapace, consisting of cartilaginous material located at the junction of the second and third costal (side) laminae, or about in the middle of the shell. This gives the tortoise the ability to completely tuck in its hind feet and tail when threatened. Hingeback tortoises have brown carapaces and yellow heads; they grow to a maximum length of about 13 inches (33 centimeters).

EUROPEAN TORTOISES

Five species of tortoises, all of the genus *Testudo*, are found in Europe and areas surrounding the Mediterranean Sea. One of the best-known is the Mediterranean spur-thigh tortoise (*Testudo graeca*), which lives in North Africa, the Near East, and extreme southern Europe. It has a moderately domed carapace 7 to 8 inches (18 to 20 centimeters) in length, of a dull yellow or olive color. The anterior portion of each lamina has a black border, and each thigh has a prominent spur. The spur-thigh tortoise hibernates in cold weather; females normally lay only two or three eggs per clutch.

This tortoise has been the most popular pet tortoise in Britain; at one time, 300,000 per year were shipped from Morocco to

Top: The African pancake tortoise, which wedges itself between rocks to escape danger. *Bottom:* The radiated tortoise of Madagascar. Its meat is believed by some natives to have aphrodisiac properties.

Above, top: The Chilean or Chaco tortoise *(Geochelone chilensis),* a South American species taken as a pet and also used for food. *Above, bottom:* The Indian star tortoise *(Testudo radiata),* an exotic species closely related to the leopard tortoise.

England. Unfortunately, upward of 90 percent died within a year, because the British climate was too cold and damp for them. Under appropriate conditions, this tortoise can live to be very old—some have lived for more than 100 years.

Hermann's tortoise (*Testudo hermanni*) is found only in Europe (southern Italy, Sicily, Yugoslavia, Albania, Bulgaria, Turkey, and Rumania). It is very similar in appearance to *Testudo graeca,* except that it lacks thigh spurs and is smaller. Hermann's tortoise, which has a sharp spine on the tip of its tail, is also popular as a pet turtle.

The largest member of the genus is the margined tortoise (*Testudo marginata*), which is found only in southern Greece. It grows to 12 inches (30 centimeters) in length, with an elongated shell and flared marginals at the back of the carapace of males.

ASIAN TORTOISES

Seven species of tortoises, all genus *Geochelone,* live in India, Celebes, and Southeast Asia; one (the starred tortoise of India, *Geochelone elegans*), has been mentioned. Another, the Burmese brown tortoise (*Geochelone emys*) is considered one of the two most primitive living tortoises (that is, resembling emydids, from which tortoises are derived) because of its flattened shell and preference for living in moist, tropical forests, among other qualities. The Burmese brown tortoise is the largest of the Asian tortoises (with a maximum carapace length of 18 inches [46 centimeters]) and lives in Burma, Thailand, the Malay Peninsula, Sumatra, and Borneo. It is prized as a food source throughout its range.

SOUTH AMERICAN TORTOISES

In mainland South America, there are three species of tortoises, again all genus *Geochelone,* which are very abundant and range over virtually the entire continent: the yellow-footed tortoise (*Geochelone denticulata*), the red-footed tortoise (*Geochelone carbonaria*), and the Chaco or Argentine tortoise (*Geochelone chilensis*).

© Gerry Ellis/Ellis Wildlife Collection

The yellow-footed tortoise, sometimes known as the Hercules, jaboty, or Brazilian giant tortoise, is found in the dense rain forests and tropical lowlands of South America. Sexual differences are pronounced in this species: Females grow to a length of 2 or 2½ feet (60 to 76 centimeters), while males rarely exceed 16 inches (40 centimeters). The shape of the carapace is different, too: Males have long, low shells with a deeply concave plastron; females have high, narrow shells with a flat plastron.

In mature turtles of both sexes, the shell is thick and heavy—dark brown with patches of yellow on each scute. The plastron is also dark brown, and the limbs and head are brown with some orange scales and markings.

Yellow-footed tortoises live hidden in the thick forest undergrowth (avoiding clearings and wide trails); they prefer a diet of leaves

© Gerry Ellis/Ellis Wildlife Collection

Above and left: The red-footed tortoise *(Geochelone carbonaria)* is a strikingly marked, medium-sized turtle found throughout South America.

and fruit, though they occasionally eat insects and will eat meat in captivity. They are highly valued as food; Pritchard reports that natives often set whole hillsides afire, then "walk through afterward and pick up the exposed (and presumably roasted) tortoises."

The closely related red-footed tortoise, which inhabits roughly the same areas as *Geochelone denticulata,* is smaller than the yellow-footed, reaching a length of about 17 inches (43 centimeters), the males being a little larger than females. The carapace is black with an indentation in the center, giving it a slightly hourglass shape when looked at from above, and there are red and reddish yellow scales on the legs and head, which are also black. Each of the laminae has some red or reddish yellow marking, too. The red-footed tortoise is found in open prairies as well as in forests.

The two above-mentioned tortoises engage in interesting courtship behavior. If a male yellow-footed encounters another yellow-footed, it walks to the side of it and then moves its head suddenly sideways, usually toward the tortoise, then quickly back to the center position. If the other tortoise is a male, it will respond similarly. If not, the first tortoise will walk to the back of the other and sniff its cloacal region to verify that it is a female. If that's the case, the male initiates copulation almost immediately. The red-footed tortoise makes slightly different head movements and emits a henlike "clucking" sound when copulating.

The range of the Chaco tortoise extends further south than that of the others; it is abundant in Argentina and Chile, sometimes reaching a population density of fifteen to twenty per acre. It grows to about 14 inches (35 centimeters) in length, and females are slightly larger than males. The carapace is yellow-brown with darker laminar edges, which is useful for camouflage. The Chaco tortoise is also used for food and is considered an endangered species by some authorities.

NORTH AMERICAN TORTOISES

All four North American tortoises belong to the genus *Gopherus*: the gopher tortoise, the desert tortoise, the Texas tortoise, and the Bolson tortoise.

The gopher tortoise (*Gopherus polyphemus*) is distributed over the largest geographical area—Florida, southern Mississippi, Alabama, the southern half of Georgia, and extreme eastern Louisiana—though none of the four tortoises lives in a particularly large area, and no species' territory overlaps another's.

The gopher tortoise usually grows to slightly less than a foot in length (the record is about 16 inches [40 centimeters]) and a weight of 29 pounds (11 kilograms). Its carapace is brown with well-defined annular rings, and the plastron is yellow. Also, the hind feet are comparatively small.

"Gophers" have two distinct physical characteristics: The gular laminae (the foremost laminae of the plastron) normally extend quite far forward under the neck and chin of the tortoise (males use them as battering rams), and their forelimbs are flattened, with rigid wrists.

The latter feature gives the gopher tortoise the ability to engage in the activity from which it derives its name: to dig long burrows that become its home at night and during periods of cold weather.

Gophers often live in the transitional zones between two ecosystems, such as woodland and pasture. They begin burrow-

The South American yellow-footed tortoise (*Geochelone denticulata*), known as "jaboty" in Brazil. A vegetarian, this tortoise lives in dense rain forests and is prized as a food source by humans.

© Zoological Society of San Diego

ing, typically in loose or sandy soil, from the time they are hatchlings; they are quite territorial, and a tortoise may inhabit a single burrow for most of its life, never roaming far from it. Burrows may be as long as 30 feet (9 meters) and as deep as 12 feet (3.6 meters); they may be straight or curved and may have an enlarged chamber in them. Gopher tortoises are active year round and only hibernate briefly during very cold periods.

A burrow provides the tortoise with an easy escape from the hot sun; the temperature in the burrow is more constant and the humidity greater. Normally, gopher tortoises emerge from their burrows when the day begins to get warm. They feed on nearby leaves and grasses, sometimes along well-defined "grazing trails." Usually, they return in the early afternoon. If disturbed or frightened near its burrow, a gopher tortoise will head rapidly toward it and wedge itself inside by extending its feet and head.

Other animals frequently share the burrows of gopher tortoises. These include beetles, cave crickets, spiders, lizards, gopher frogs, gopher mice, and an occasional snake. None of these cause the gopher tortoise any benefit or harm, though sometimes tortoises die when humans, trying to flush out rattlesnakes, pour gasoline down gopher holes and set them afire.

When courting, male gopher tortoises walk in a circle around females, bobbing their heads up and down to attract them; for some reason, this seems to work. Next, males bite females on the legs and on the front edge of their shells to encourage submissiveness and immobility, upon which mating commences. Females make nests from April through July, normally laying four to seven eggs.

Though skunks, raccoons, and snakes destroy nests and eat hatchlings, human beings are the principal killer of adult gopher tortoises: encroaching upon their territory with housing developments, agriculture, and shopping centers; running over tortoises on the road; and, before the gopher tortoise was protected, capturing adults and juveniles for use as pets, where they do poorly and rarely survive.

The desert tortoise (*Gopherus agassizi*) lives in southern Nevada, southeastern California, western Arizona, and extreme south-

© A.B. Sheldon

western Utah in the United States, plus northern Baja California, western Sonora, and northwestern Sinaloa in Mexico. It is about the same size and color as the gopher tortoise, with prominent growth rings on the carapace and elongated gular laminae. Sometimes there are yellow or orange patches in the center of each lamina. Its hind feet are larger than those of the gopher tortoise, however, and its head is narrower.

The habitat of the desert tortoise is more severe than that of the gopher tortoise—temperatures are both hotter and colder, the humidity is lower and there is less water available—so it must live its life differently.

In northern regions, the desert tortoise has both a "summer" and a "winter" range. In summer, because it tolerates heat well, the desert tortoise wanders over arid, flat desert

The Florida gopher tortoise *(Gopherus polyphemus)* is a distant relative of the desert tortoise.

and dry stream beds, retiring at night to shallow burrows (2 to 4 feet [60 centimeters to 1.2 meters] deep) it digs in gravelly or sandy soil near the base of shrubs. In winter, in order to survive periods of extreme cold, it hibernates in the foothills (sometimes communally) in larger, deeper burrows (15 feet [4.5 meters] long or more, dug in hard ground). At the southern extremes of its range, it has no need to burrow at all.

The desert tortoise is herbivorous, eating grasses, leaves, cactus pads, and desert flowers. Usually, it forages actively in the early morning and late afternoon. Because it lives in such dry climates, the desert tortoise is capable of going for a year or more without drinking water. It is also able to store and reabsorb water from its bladder, excreting nitrogenous wastes in the form of semi-solid urates instead of urinating.

The mating habits of the desert tortoise are similar to those of the gopher tortoise. Male desert tortoises are aggressive toward one another, frequently fighting, especially during mating season (spring and early summer). The desert tortoise reaches sexual maturity slowly (fifteen to twenty years).

As is the case with the gopher tortoise, the desert tortoise makes a poor pet, requiring specialized care. Desert tortoises are protected in the United States as an endangered species by the U.S. Fish and Wildlife Service. Still, many are run over on the roads and deserts by cars and off-road vehicles, many are still taken as pets, many must compete (unsuccessfully) with cattle for food, and many are cruelly used for target practice.

The Texas tortoise (*Gopherus berlandieri*) is the smallest of the four species found in North America; it grows to a length of only 6 or 7 inches (15 or 18 centimeters). It lives in the southern one-third of Texas, plus the Mexican states of Coahuila, Nuevo Leon, and Tamaulipas.

It has a rounded, brown shell with yellow patches and extended, forked gular laminae. As the Texas tortoise ages, its shell lightens to a uniform tan or bone color. The Texas tortoise rarely digs a burrow; at most, it scoops out a shallow depression in the sand for protection. Like the desert tortoise, it feeds on grass, cactus pads, flowers, and fruit; sometimes it eats beetles and land snails.

© Manny Rubio

Man is by far the chief destroyer of the Texas tortoise. Although the state of Texas has passed legislation protecting it from being harmed or taken as a pet, quite a few are still collected for the pet industry. This is unfortunate, because the species is only slightly more hardy than the desert and gopher tortoise, and it has a low reproductive potential, usually laying only one or two eggs per clutch.

The Bolson tortoise or giant Mexican gopher tortoise (*Gopherus flavomarginatus*), was only recently (1959) categorized as a separate species. It lives in a small region of north-central Mexico; typically, it may mature to about 1 foot (30 centimeters) in length, but a number of individuals have been recorded with a carapace length exceeding 2 feet (60 centimeters). It has a pale yellow or straw-colored carapace when young, turning pale brown in adults.

The Bolson tortoise digs burrows ranging from 10 to 20 feet (3 to 6 meters) long. Like the gopher tortoise, it feeds along grazing paths in the early morning and late afternoon, retiring to its burrow at midday and at night. Bolson tortoises are slowly being exterminated as people move onto the land or plant crops on the lands the tortoise inhabits. It is also hunted for food and sometimes killed simply because people think the tortoise competes with cattle for sparse grass.

Opposite page: California's state reptile, the desert tortoise *(Gopherus agassizi)* is now fully protected by legislation as an endangered species. *Above:* The desert tortoise is nomadic in its habits, traveling long distances from summer to winter to adapt to the extreme range of temperatures.

SIDE-NECKED TURTLES

The basic distinction between turtles depends on whether they retract their head straight back into their shell (straight-necked turtles) or by lateral flexion, laying it sideways in the groove between the carapace and plastron, next to a front foot (side-necks). These two groups (suborders) are known as Cryptodira and Pleurodira, respectively.

Most turtles in the world—the turtles we have been describing, nearly 150 species—belong to the suborder Cryptodira, or straight-necked turtles. No discussion of turtles would be complete, however, without a description of some of the two families (Pelomedusidae and Chelidae) and about sixty species that make up the suborder Pleurodira—the side-necked turtles. Some of the most unusual and interesting turtles in the world are side-necks.

Side-necked turtles are considered less physiologically advanced than straight-necked turtles, because a threatened side-necked turtle can only protect itself by pushing its head further into its shoulder, leaving one side of its neck and head exposed. The other major distinction between straight-necked and side-necked turtles is that the pelvic bones of side-necks are fused to both the carapace and plastron, while in straight-necked turtles there is no bony connection.

Seventy million years ago, side-necked turtles inhabited the globe on both sides of the equator. Today, they live only in the southern hemisphere—South America, sub-Saharan Africa, and Madagascar—and are the only non-marine turtles in Australia.

The largest of all side-necks of the family Pelomedusidae (five genera, about twenty-four species) is the arrau river turtle (*Podocnemis expansa*) which lives in the Amazon River system of South America.

The carapace of the arrau turtle is flat and brown, the plastron gray; the head is black with yellow markings and a pointed snout.

Large females grow to a carapace length of 3 feet (1 meter) and a weight of 200 pounds (75 kilograms), although the average size for females is 2 feet (73 centimeters) in length and 70 pounds (26 kilograms). Males are smaller and less numerous than females.

The arrau is similar in many respects to sea turtles; it is large and aquatic, it shows a preference for congregating at night in a few favored places to nest, and it lays many eggs (upward of 100). Also, like many sea turtles, arrau turtles may only nest every three or four years (though laying several clutches in that year). Adults are strictly herbivorous.

For more than 150 years, the arrau turtle has been heavily exploited by natives: Large numbers of adults are killed for food, and eggs are taken for food and other purposes (oil in the eggs is used for lighting, cooking, and lubrication).

In the past forty years, the arrau population has declined significantly: For example, it was estimated that in 1800, a favored nesting beach was used by 330,000 turtles;

in 1945, the number had dropped to 123,000; in 1956, to 36,000; and in 1969, to just under 14,000. The arrau river turtle is now an officially endangered species, but it is protected only sporadically.

Another prominent side-neck is the Amazon yellow-spotted turtle (*Podocnemis unifilis*). Somewhat similar in appearance to the arrau river turtle, the Amazon yellow-spotted turtle has a higher dome on its carapace and typically grows to a carapace length of about 15 inches (38 centimeters). It tends to inhabit ponds and lakes more than rivers.

More species of Pelomedusid side-necks live in Africa than anywhere else in the world. The side-neck with the greatest range is probably the helmeted turtle (*Pelomedusa subrufa*), which is found over most of the continent south of the Sahara. It has an olive-brown carapace and a yellowish plastron (though it lacks a plastral hinge); it typically grows to slightly less than a foot (36 centimeters) in length.

A gathering of teracays, or Amazon yellow-spotted turtles (*Podocnemis unifilis*), a South American side-neck once popular in the pet trade.

North Wind Picture Archive

The helmeted turtle is semiaquatic, mostly carnivorous, and lays relatively large clutches of eggs (fifteen to forty). It likes to bask and has been observed doing so on the backs of hippopotamuses. The helmeted turtle was once heavily imported for the pet trade in Europe.

A number of other side-necked turtles live in sub-Saharan Africa. A dozen or so species belong to the genus *Pelusios,* which is distinguished by a hinge across the plastron, allowing the front portion to be raised as a protection for the head and forelimbs.

The other family of side-necked turtles, Chelidae, is composed of nine or ten genera and thirty-five to forty species, which are found in South America and Australia only. This family is considered more advanced than the Pelomedusidae, because parts of the carapace and skull are more specialized and resemble those of cryptodiran turtles.

Eight species of side-necks known as snake-necked turtles live in Australia. As their name suggests, snake-necked turtles have extremely long necks—sometimes the length of the head and neck is nearly that of the carapace. Snake-necked turtles are aquatic or semiaquatic.

The most familiar and widespread of the snake-necks is known simply as the Australian snake-necked turtle (*Chelodina longicollis*); it inhabits much of southwestern Australia (portions of the states of South Australia, Victoria, New South Wales, and Queensland). Adults grow to a carapace

An arrau river turtle, a large South American side-neck valued as a food source by native tribes.

length of about 7 inches (21 centimeters), with 12 inches (37 centimeters) as the maximum. Its shell is brown or black and has a wrinkled texture. The neck is dark on top, with a warty appearance; the head is slender, with a bright, staring eye, which gives it a bizarre, somewhat threatening look.

The Australian snake-necked turtle eats frogs, tadpoles, aquatic insects, and occasionally fish. When a newly caught turtle is picked up, it usually emits a strong-smelling liquid from glands near the rear legs. In captivity, however, the Australian snake-necked turtle becomes docile and friendly.

The largest of the Australian chelids is the snake-necked turtle known as *Chelodina expansa,* a river-dweller that lives in Queensland, New South Wales, and Victoria. It normally grows to a carapace length of 11 inches (34 centimeters); the largest specimens have been measured at nearly 17 inches (52 centimeters). The head of *C. expansa* is flat and wide; its diet is similar to that of *C. longicollis.*

Another snake-necked turtle worth mentioning is *Chelodina oblonga,* which lives in the swamps and streams of a large section of southwest Western Australia. Its neck is longer (relatively) than that of any other turtle species and is so thick and muscular that it is impossible for the turtle to draw it

© Bayard H Brattstrom/Visuals Unlimited

into its shell. When the turtle walks, it holds its long neck and head straight out in front of the shell.

Another well-known Australian side-neck is the Murray River turtle (*Emydura macquarrii*), the most numerous species of its genus; it is found throughout the Murray River and its tributaries (in southern South Australia, New South Wales, and Victoria) and in other parts of western Australia.

The Murray River turtle grows to a maximum length of about 13 inches (40 centimeters); its relatively flat shell is very broad in juveniles, becoming oval as the animal matures. The shell is medium brown and has a wrinkled appearance. The Murray River turtle's head is small, with a pointed snout and bright, prominent eyes; usually, the head has a pair of barbels (cone-shaped projections) on the chin.

Frogs, tadpoles, and aquatic vegetation make up the Murray River turtle's diet. Apart from the fact that it is numerous, the most noteworthy quality about the Murray River turtle is its energetic, somewhat hostile temperament—it has an inclination to inflict painful bites on anyone attempting to capture or handle it. It is said to retain this disposition even in captivity.

Two species of snake-necked turtles are found in South America, although they belong to a different genus, *Hydromedusa*. The most plentiful and widely distributed is named *Hydromedusa tectifera*, a turtle that grows to a carapace length of 12 inches (36 centimeters) and inhabits parts of Argentina, Uruguay, Paraguay, and southern Brazil. Its carapace is dark brown or black, with a yellow-brown plastron. The top of the neck, head, and limbs is dark gray; the underside of the head is pale yellow with small, gray spots. Females grow to a larger size than males.

Little is known about the habits of *Hydromedusa tectifera*. It is said to be nervous and shy, retaining these qualities even in captivity. Its preferred food is snails, though it also eats tadpoles and aquatic insects.

Without a doubt, the most unusual turtle in the world—side-necked or straight-necked—is the famous matamata turtle (*Chelus fimbriatus*), an aquatic species that inhabits much of the Amazon and Orinoco river systems in northern South America.

© Erika Klass

The Australian matamata *(Chelus fimbriatus),* perhaps the most bizarre-looking turtle in the world.

So strange is the matamata that it barely looks like a turtle at all; it resembles a pile of debris. The matamata's carapace reaches a length of about 16 inches (49 centimeters), and the turtle has an extremely long, muscular neck. Its flattened, triangular head has a long snout, small eyes, and wide jaws with weak jaw muscles. Its limbs are small and weak.

The matamata's long carapace and neck is extremely rough and uneven in texture, and the head is covered with shreds and filaments of skin. Adult matamatas are dark brown or black, while younger turtles are often a more colorful brown and yellow mix, like fallen leaves. Adults often have a thick covering of algae on the carapace, which contributes to their camouflaged appearance.

The matamata leads a sedentary, but predatory, way of life, much like that of the alligator snapping turtle. It lies on the bottom of ponds and slow-moving streams and rivers, occasionally stretching its long neck to the surface to breathe. But mostly it just waits for small fish to come near; the fish nibble on fibrous parts of its head, thinking it to be edible refuse. Then the matamata springs into action, rapidly expanding its huge mouth and neck, sucking in a large flood of water and the hapless fish. Next, the matamata opens its mouth slightly and allows the water, but not the fish, to escape. Its jaws lack horny edges for chewing, so the matamata simply swallows its food whole.

MARINE TURTLES

A number of turtle species moved from the marshes and land back to the sea early on, about 150 million years ago. By 100 million years ago, four families of marine turtles inhabited the planet.

Marine turtles differ from semiaquatic turtles and tortoises in a number of their anatomical features. One of the most obvious is that the feet of marine turtles take the form of flippers—the digits are fused so the flippers function like efficient paddles, enabling marine turtles to move gracefully and rapidly through the water. Each flipper has only one or two claws, except for that of the leatherback, which has none.

Internally, the bony structure of the carapace and plastron is reduced in marine turtles, and the shell is streamlined. Marine turtles are unable to withdraw their necks and heads into their shells (to compensate, they have completely roofed-over skulls, which offer their vulnerable heads better protection). All species have glands that collect and excrete excessive salt from their blood.

Marine turtles inhabit all temperate and tropical oceans, spending virtually all their time in the water. Only female marine turtles leave the sea, when they come ashore to nest; a male may never leave the ocean in its entire lifetime—perhaps half a century. Because of this, we know relatively little of marine turtles' movements, navigational ability, or their development from infancy to maturity.

All species of marine turtles are capable of living on the high seas, and though some species (the green turtle, for instance) travel great distances between their feeding and nesting grounds, most spend the majority of their time in the warmer, shallower waters near the shorelines of continents and islands. This makes it easier to find food and mates. Only the leatherback and olive ridley spend much of their time in the open ocean.

Marine turtles eat both animal and vegetable foods. Seagrasses and algae are the most important vegetation; animal prey includes crabs, snails, jellyfish, mussels, and rarely small fish. All marine turtles are large (total length: 3 to 7 feet [1 to 2 meters]) and

hence, as adults, have few enemies except man, although occasionally sharks or killer whales attack them.

The shells of adult marine turtles, with the exception of green turtles, typically become covered with all sorts of organisms, including seaweed, barnacles, crustaceans, and leeches. Remora—fish that frequently attach themselves by suction to sharks—also allow themselves to be carried along by marine turtles.

MIGRATION AND MATING

Over the past three decades, researchers have tagged marine turtles with metal or plastic identification markers in an attempt to chart their patterns of migration. They have learned that turtles migrate between specific beaches and feeding grounds.

What we do not understand is how turtles that migrate over great stretches of open ocean find their way from place to place. For instance, how does a female green turtle find her way back to the beach where she was hatched decades before, so that she may lay her eggs? As Pritchard says, "... the feat of locating Ascension Island, barely seven miles across, after negotiating 1,400 miles of open ocean, by an animal that is hopelessly myopic when it raises its eyes above the level of the water, seems little short of miraculous."

Scientists think that the turtle's senses of smell, taste, and sight must be involved:

The loggerhead *(Caretta caretta)* is so named for its relatively large head. It is found in the Atlantic, Pacific, and Indian oceans, as well as the Mediterranean Sea.

Hatchlings smell or nibble the sand on their way to the nest, as if attempting to imprint its scent or taste upon their senses. Likewise, adult green turtles and ridleys appear to test the sand when they crawl onto a beach to nest. Perhaps, like bees, turtles have a sun-compass sense and are able to use the sun and stars to guide themselves—we just don't know.

Marine turtles mate offshore, then the females emerge from the sea to lay their eggs. Depending on the species, a turtle may nest up to six times (at two-week intervals) in a season, mating in between nestings. Many marine turtles rarely nest every year—two- to three-year intervals are typical.

Nesting generally takes place at night. Females drag themselves out of the surf and move laboriously as much as 100 yards (91 meters) up the beach, out of reach of the highest tides. Initially, many species are very skittish and will return to the sea at the slightest noise or sound.

When she has selected a site, she begins to dig a nest with her hind flippers in the more densely packed sand under her tail. While she is digging, "tears" flow from her eyes to eliminate excess salt from her system and wash away any sand that has accumulated.

Depending on the size of the turtle, the egg cavity might be from 1 to 2½ feet (36 to 91 centimeters) deep. Once the nest has been dug, the female lays her eggs—each about 2 inches (6 centimeters) in diameter, anywhere from fifty to 200 in number—singly or in groups of three or four, in intervals of eight to twelve seconds. She folds her flippers up out of the way and lets the eggs drop directly onto the sand.

The total egg-laying process usually takes from fifteen to thirty minutes. At this time, females are especially vulnerable, because once a turtle begins laying her eggs, almost nothing can dissuade her, even the presence of people or predators. She is in an almost trancelike state, focused only on this. To complete the process, the turtle covers the nest with sand, flinging it around with both flippers and flattening the whole area with her body.

Afterward, it is difficult to determine the location of the nest itself. Then, often nearly exhausted, the female drags herself—perhaps pausing several times to rest—to the surf and disappears into the ocean.

Predators (human beings, coyotes, wild dogs, and feral hogs) seem to know when and where turtles will come ashore to nest, and they await the turtles' arrival. As well, humans take the eggs and sometimes kill the turtles as they are nesting.

Additionally, humans and killer whales often attack male and female turtles while they are mating. Raccoons and skunks, using their sense of smell, destroy nests and eat the eggs. If a turtle's nest can survive a couple of days, though, the female's scent usually diminishes sufficiently and the nest is safe.

After varying periods of incubation (two to two-and-a-half months is typical), baby turtles burst from the nest, usually at night. Focusing on the reflection of light off the water, they head for the sea. Again, the predators—gulls, ravens, ghost crabs, sharks, groupers—are there, waiting for a meal of young turtles. Many are eaten in the first few days of life.

Once in the water, the hatchlings enter what are referred to as "the lost years," that indeterminate period of time when humans rarely see them. On one occasion in the late 1980s, near the end of his life, Archie Carr watched dozens of newly hatched sea turtles scramble from their nest and dash pell-mell toward the ocean, vanishing in the surf. "Where are they going?" he said. "I wish I

The largest and most widely distributed of the hard-shell marine turtles, the green turtle (Chelonia mydas) is famous for its extensive migrations.

© Chris Huss/Ellis Wildlife Collection

knew. I've spent a lot of time working on that problem, and so have a lot of other people."

Turtle experts think that, somehow, most hatchlings make their way to rafts of seaweed and sargassum, feeding and drifting with the currents until they become large enough and strong enough to travel through the ocean. How many survive to maturity? Estimates vary: A reasonable guess is one per thousand.

THE SEVEN SPECIES

Currently, there are two families of marine turtles: Cheloniidae, with six species (the green turtle, flatback, loggerhead, hawksbill, Kemp's ridley and olive ridley); and Dermochelyidae, with a single species (the leatherback).

The most abundant of marine turtles is the green turtle (*Chelonia mydas*), which inhabits the Atlantic, Pacific, and Indian oceans, plus the Mediterranean Sea. Its primary nesting beaches are located in Central

and South America, Asia, Australia, Indonesia, Hawaii, Ascension Island (in the Atlantic Ocean), and Europa Island (near Madagascar).

As mentioned above, green turtles are famous for their extensive migrations; for example, green turtles who feed off the coast of Brazil swim to Ascension Island, 1,400 miles (2,240 kilometers) away, to make their nests.

The green turtle is the largest of the hardshell marine turtles. Typically it grows to a carapace length of about 40 inches (1 meter) and a weight of 300 to 350 pounds (110 to 130 kilograms), although individuals measuring about 55 inches (1.7 meters) and weighing close to 500 pounds (187 kilograms) have been recorded.

The carapace of the green turtle is smooth, heart-shaped, and, in adults, medium brown or olive in color; the green turtle gets its name from the color of its calipee (belly cartilage), which is used to make turtle soup. The plastron is light yellow, its head is small, its snout is rounded, and its eyes are prominent.

The green turtle (*Chelonia mydas*) is the largest of the hard-shelled sea turtles. Found in all oceans, the green turtle has been called "the archetypical marine turtle" by Peter Pritchard and "the most valuable reptile in the world " by Archie Carr.

The green turtle feeds mostly on seagrasses and marine algae. Its serrated lower jaw is well-suited for this, but it also has been reported to eat crustaceans, jellyfish, and sponges. Juveniles may be more carnivorous than adults.

Green turtle meat and eggs have been an important source of food for native populations; Europeans and Americans consider green turtle steaks a delicacy. As a result, whole populations of green turtles have been decimated, and today the species is classified as endangered by the IUCN *Red Data Book*.

At one time, for instance, the green turtle nested in great numbers on beaches in Florida, but now in the United States only a handful of females nest on a small section of beach in Florida. In Indonesia, 36 million eggs were collected in 1936; between 1967 and 1972, the average number taken was only 320,000.

The flatback turtle (*Natator depressus*), lives off the beaches of northern Australia. The flatback is small (typically: 30 inches [91 centimeters] and 160 pounds [60 kilograms]) and has a flattened carapace with turned-up edges. Its head is relatively larger and more triangularly shaped than that of the green turtle, and its front flippers are relatively shorter.

Little is known of the flatback's behavior, migrations, or feeding habits. It lays fewer eggs (fifty in a typical clutch) than any other marine turtle, but the eggs are larger than those of any but the leatherback's, to which they are equal in size. Pritchard says that this gives the flatback hatchlings, which are 50 percent larger than green turtle or loggerhead hatchlings, a better chance of surviving attacks by gulls and ghost crabs. Monitor lizards and foxes destroy flatback nests.

Another large marine turtle is the loggerhead (*Caretta caretta*), which is named for its large, broad head. Loggerheads typically grow to a carapace length of 3 feet (1 meter) and a weight of 200 to 350 pounds (75 to 130 kilograms). Its carapace is reddish brown, and its plastron is yellow-orange.

Loggerheads live in the Atlantic (nesting in Florida), the Mediterranean, the Indian Ocean (off southern Africa and Madagascar), and the Pacific (near Japan, China, Australia, and Mexico).

Typically, the loggerhead nests far from rather than close to the equator: just north of the Tropic of Cancer and just south of the Tropic of Capricorn. Like the green turtle, the loggerhead is an extensive traveler.

Loggerheads are omnivorous, but prefer a diet of meat: crabs, conches, urchins, jellyfish, squid, barnacles, sponges, and fish. They will, however, eat small quantities of seaweed. Loggerheads are reputed to be hostile and aggressive when captured, capable of inflicting considerable damage on fishing boats and their crews.

At one time, loggerheads were prized for their meat and eggs. This is still true in some underdeveloped countries, but in many developed countries, including the United States, the species is listed as threatened and is therefore protected. Today, the largest single cause of loggerhead mortality is accidental drowning in shrimp trawls.

The hawksbill (*Eretmochelys imbricata*) gets its name from its long, narrow head and snout, which tapers to a point. It lives mostly in tropical waters—the Caribbean (Cuba, Panama, and Costa Rica), north of Madagascar, Indonesia, and off the northeast coast of Australia.

Smaller than the green turtle, flatback, and loggerhead, the hawksbill varies in size depending on where it is found. Those in the Caribbean typically grow to a carapace length of 2½ to 3 feet (76 to 91 centimeters) and weigh from 100 to 165 pounds (45 to 75 kilograms); Asian and Pacific hawksbills range in size from 2 to 2½ feet (61 to 76 centimeters) and 75 to 110 pounds (28 to 41 kilograms). The carapace of the hawksbill is heart-shaped, like that of the green turtle, and ranges in color from amber to dark brown or dark green. The head and limbs are dark brown or black on the upper surfaces; underneath, they are whitish yellow or yellow-orange, as is the plastron.

The hawksbill is omnivorous, though it prefers a diet of marine invertebrates, such as mollusks, crustaceans, sea urchins, jellyfish, and sponges. Young hawksbills are generally herbivorous, becoming more carnivorous as they mature.

On the average, hawksbills lay more eggs than other sea turtles, about 160 per clutch in Caribbean nests. Unlike some other marine species, which nest in large numbers, hawksbills frequently nest alone or in small groups. This makes it difficult to learn much about their habits and behavior.

Opposite page: The loggerhead (*Caretta caretta*) has a long, reddish brown carapace and a large head. *Overleaf:* One of the smaller sea turtles, the hawksbill (*Eretmochelys imbricata*) is prized for its colorful scutes, the source of tortoiseshell products. Juveniles are also stuffed and mounted as decoration for homes and offices in the Orient.

© Manny Rubio

A green turtle *(Chelonia mydas [bottom of photo])* and a hawksbill *(top of photo).*

Although it is eaten only infrequently, the hawksbill is prized the world over for its beautiful scutes, known incorrectly as "tortoiseshell." Thick and overlapping, the horny scutes are translucent with radiating streaks of reddish brown and black when peeled from the carapace and polished.

Juvenile hawksbills are imported to Japan from Indonesia, where they are stuffed, lacquered, and hung on the walls of many Japanese residences, ironically as a symbol of longevity. About 10,000 young hawksbills per year meet this fate in the Orient, and the same practice takes place in Mexico. The hawksbill is considered endangered, and Pritchard describes the species as "universally heavily exploited."

The smallest, rarest, and most endangered of marine turtles is the Kemp's ridley (*Lepidochelys kempii*), which lives only in the Gulf of Mexico and the shallow, coastal waters of the eastern United States. It has a broad carapace that seldom grows beyond a length of 2½ feet (76 centimeters) and a weight of 80 to 120 pounds (30 to 45 kilograms). The carapace, skin, and plastron are gray in hatchlings, but as the turtle matures, the plastron, neck, and underside of the shoulders become pale yellow and the carapace sometimes becomes olive green.

Kemp's ridleys prefer a largely carnivorous diet, eating crabs, shrimp, clams, lobster, jellyfish, and snails.

The Kemp's ridley is reputed to respond with extreme violence and hysteria when attempts are made to capture it, thrashing and snapping itself to exhaustion. In captivity, Kemp's ridleys become more calm but never entirely lose their nervous dispositions.

The most unusual quality about the Kemp's ridley is its nesting behavior, which was unknown to the scientific world until 1963. It nests primarily in one place in the world, on a remote beach near the village of Rancho Nuevo in Tamaulipas, Mexico, about 200 miles (320 kilometers) south of Brownsville, Texas. Ridleys gather in the waters offshore and swarm onto the beach all at the same time, during the day (rather than at night, when most marine turtles nest).

This event, known locally as an *arribada* (arrival or aggregation), takes place three times a season, at intervals of a few weeks in the months of April through June, on a slightly different section of beach each time.

Mexican natives have known about arribadas for a long time; the event serves as a convenient way for them to obtain turtle meat and eggs. The outside world learned of arribadas by accident, however. A local resident, Andres Herrera, filmed an arribada in 1947, but only a few people ever saw the film until more than a decade later. It shows thousands of turtles coming ashore; the best estimate is that perhaps 40,000 nested in a single day.

An indication of how much the Kemp's ridley has been exploited in recent years is the fact that although the Mexican government has protected the arribadas against poachers since 1966, sometimes with armed soldiers, the population of nesting Kemp's ridleys continues to decline. In recent years, only about 400 females per season have come to Rancho Nuevo to nest.

The other largest single enemy of the Kemp's ridley is the shrimp trawler—750 Kemp's ridleys per year are drowned in shrimpers' nets.

Slightly larger than the Kemp's ridley is the olive ridley (*Lepidochelys olivacea*), which inhabits tropical waters of the Pacific, Indian, and South Atlantic oceans. It has a thinner, narrower carapace that is uniformly olive in color, and a smaller, more lightly built skull with less-muscular jaws. Unlike Kemp's ridleys, olive ridleys do not restrict themselves just to coastal waters, but rather swim far out into the ocean. The diet of the olive ridley is similar to that of the Kemp's ridley, except that it does not include as many hard-shelled invertebrates.

Olive ridleys, too, participate in arribadas, though they generally nest at night. Nesting sites are located in the south Atlantic in Surinam and Costa Rica, at several locations on the west coast of Mexico, and on the coast at Orissa, India. Nesting takes place in almost every month of the year, depending on location. The largest arribada on record occurred in 1968, on the Pacific coast at Escobilla, Oaxaca, Mexico, and involved an estimated 80,000 turtles.

Several decades ago, Mexican natives heavily exploited the eggs of the olive ridley and its population began to decline. Now, because it is listed as a threatened species, the turtle and its eggs are protected.

The largest marine turtle—in fact, the largest reptile in the world—is the leatherback (*Dermochelys coriacea*). It is so markedly different from other sea turtles in its physiology (though not in its habits) that it is placed in another family, Dermochelyidae, of which it is the sole species.

The most obvious difference about the leatherback is that its huge, barrel-shaped body has no shell; instead, it has a leathery, scaleless skin over a thick, greasy layer of cartilage, in which is imbedded a mosaic of thousands of small, polygonal bones.

The leatherback has paddlelike, clawless flippers; massive, muscular shoulders and neck; a large, smooth head with relatively weak, scissorlike jaws; and tender skin on its neck and legs. Males have concave plastrons, slightly depressed, tapering carapaces, and tails that are considerably longer than those of females.

The leatherback's carapace is black, with longitudinal ridges. Its whitish plastron also has five longitudinal ridges. The head and limbs are the same color as the carapace. Sometimes the carapace and flippers are dotted with white spots. Leatherbacks grow to a carapace length of 5 to 7 feet (1.5 to 2 meters) and a weight of 700 to 1,600 pounds (260 to 600 kilograms). The largest leatherback recorded, a male, washed up on a beach in Wales in 1988; it weighed 2,016 pounds (750 kilograms).

Except for its nesting activity, very little is known of the migrations, diet, and behavior of the leatherback. An accomplished deep-sea swimmer, it is the most wide-ranging of marine turtles. Leatherbacks have been spotted in all oceans, frequently far out of sight of land; sometimes leatherbacks travel in groups of up to 100 turtles.

Although for the most part it inhabits temperate and tropical waters, the leatherback has the metabolic capacity to raise its body temperature above that of the water it swims in, enabling it to inhabit waters too cold for other marine turtles (for instance, off the coasts of Iceland, Canada, and Argentina). It is not known whether leatherbacks migrate or simply roam the seas. Leatherbacks specialize on a diet of jellyfish.

Leatherbacks nest at various times on beaches all over the world: both coasts of Florida, Jamaica, French Guiana, Nicaragua, Costa Rica, and on the west coast of South Africa in the Atlantic; Natal, Ceylon, India, Thailand, Malaysia, Australia, and Mexico in the Pacific. Nesting takes place individually or in small groups. During a season, leatherbacks lay eggs, on the average, more frequently than other sea turtles (as many as nine times, at ten-day intervals), though the clutch size is generally smaller (50 to 120 eggs).

Because the leatherback is such a wide-ranging "loner," it's hard to estimate how many exist. Population estimates have been revised upward in recent years, and it is now thought that there are as many as 120,000 nesting females alive. However, the fact that there seems to be an increase in the leatherback population may have more to do with the discovery of more nesting sites than with an increase in the numbers of actual turtles.

The species is still heavily exploited for its oil, although there are satisfactory synthetic substitutes for every use to which the oil is put (cosmetics, lighting, etc.). Additionally, many leatherbacks have died in recent years from intestinal blockage; it appears they have mistaken plastic bags floating in the ocean for jellyfish.

Leatherbacks do not survive in captivity. Adult leatherbacks struggle violently against any attempts at capture, smashing themselves into the sides of cages and tanks until they die. Even leatherbacks raised from hatchlings only live a year or so, at most. This most majestic of marine turtles is presently considered an endangered species.

TURTLES AND HUMANS

A TANGLED HISTORY

Considered historically and cross-culturally, the attitudes of human beings toward turtles have been widely varied and inconsistent. People have studied turtles; kept them as pets; venerated them; eaten their flesh and made use of their eggs, oil, and skin; ignored them; labored in their behalf; and thoughtlessly abused and exploited them.

We have treated turtles, alternately, as respected fellow creatures of the Earth and, to borrow an expression from Shakespeare, as "blocks, stones, and worse than senseless things." For their part, turtles have left us alone, asking nothing except to be allowed to live their lives undisturbed.

In his book *Reptiles,* Archie Carr said: "It has taken some 150 million years of paleontological disasters to reduce the immense diversity of reptilian life to a meager four orders. But it has taken man only a few hundred years of indiscriminate slaughtering to bring many survivors to the brink of complete extinction." This statement certainly applies to a significant number of turtle species.

This chapter will assess the present state of affairs between turtles and humans. On a superficial level, of course, that seems a simple enough undertaking, because in our relations with turtles we hold power over their lives, not the other way around. For us, it is natural to see the situation entirely from our perspective, describing how we view turtles and how we act toward them.

On a deeper level, however, turtles have a certain power over us: the power to reveal us as we really are, to make crystal-clear the way we see ourselves and the planet we live on, the quality of life we will bequeath to future generations, and perhaps even our very prospects for survival.

TURTLES IN MYTH AND FOLKLORE

At one time or another, the turtle has been a part of the cultural history of people in every part of the globe turtles live. Turtle images appeared on Greek coins six centuries before the birth of Christ; today, they are found on postage stamps around the world.

Turtles have played a part in the religious and artistic traditions of many cultures, too, particularly in China, Japan, and India, where turtles are represented in paintings and in sculpture.

Perhaps of even greater significance is that turtles form an important part of the folklore and myths of many societies, the psychosocial foundations from which the world view of a culture is derived.

In ancient myths and legends, the turtle is almost always greatly revered as a symbol of strength, stability, benevolence, and wisdom. Perhaps the oldest legend—in which the turtle is considered to be the second incarnation of the powerful god Vishnu—comes from India and Hinduism.

After a great flood, which occurs every four billion years and dissolves the Earth, Vishnu transforms himself into a great turtle. On his back by sheer force of will, he supports the vessel in which the gods and demons mix the elements necessary to re-create the globe. After a thousand years, when the Earth has been reborn, the turtle remains in place, and on his back stands a large elephant (or four smaller elephants, in some versions), which support the planet.

In the folklore of ancient China, Kwei, the dragon turtle, first emerged after the world was destroyed to restore order, taking charge of the creation of the heavens and earth, which required some 18,000 years. He then passed his life on to a series of guardian turtles, who were instructed to help mankind pursue truth and wisdom.

In another Chinese myth, an immense turtle actually became the world, which is contained within its body: The interior of its plastron contained the oceans upon which the continents of the Earth float, and its great, vaulted carapace formed the dome of the heavens, complete with stars and planets.

Native Americans shared the reverence felt for the turtle by Asian cultures. In fact, Native American tribes have probably created the greatest number of folk tales in which the turtle plays an important part in cosmological matters. For many tribes, the land on which they lived was the carapace of a huge "mother turtle," floating in a vast, primal sea. Almost every tribe in North America regarded one species of turtle or another as sacred. According to Archie Carr, only the Creeks took exception: They thought that box turtles caused droughts and floods, and killed them on sight.

In Central America, the Mayans gave special status to turtles, which were linked to their astronomical and mathematical systems. The Mayans depended on agriculture for their survival, and they believed that the turtle brought rain to make the crops grow. Because they observed turtles survive forest fires unharmed, the Mayans also thought that turtles have a supernatural talent for survival.

In ancient times, Egyptians generally considered the turtle to be sacred, although the Egyptian tradition apparently contained inconsistencies: In some time periods, turtles were anathema, creatures of watery darkness—the opposite of the sun god, Ra. As such, they were not to be eaten or used in any medicines; an epithet of the time stated: "May Ra live and the turtle die."

Ancient Greeks regarded the turtle as sacred and even believed that their gods felt the same way. Of course, the legendary Greek storyteller, Aesop, is given credit for the well-known fable in which a tortoise, through determination and wisdom, wins a race with a hare.

In modern times, few cultures accord the turtle any special significance. It is still held as sacred among some Asian peoples, however. One of the best-known examples is the turtles living at the Buddhist temple complex known as Wat Po, in Bangkok, Thailand. Many turtles, mostly *Hieremys annandalei,* a large black emydid turtle, live in the waters surrounding the temple.

Visitors feed fruit and vegetables to the turtles, which are regarded as symbols of immortality. The turtles are considered to be temporary dwelling places for the human souls as they make their way through a series of existences on the path to Nirvana. A similar colony of softshells (*Trionyx nigricans*) in Chittagong, Bangladesh, has already been mentioned (see page 54), although there is disagreement as to its symbolic significance.

Today, the principal interest humans have in turtles is practical or utilitarian. For example, natives living on the islands of the Seychelles Archipelago, off Madagascar in the Indian Ocean, present a newborn child with a giant Aldabran tortoise. The tortoise is raised until the child marries, then is killed and served at the wedding feast.

A Micronesian native hauls away a sea turtle to be slaughtered.

HUMAN BEINGS AND TURTLES TODAY

Turtles the world over, particularly marine turtles, are disappearing rapidly for a number of reasons: a continuing demand for turtle meat and eggs; a thriving market for tortoiseshell and leather products; accidental catching by shrimp trawlers; destruction and overdevelopment of nesting grounds by humans; and environmental pollution.

When considering the state of affairs between humans and turtles, the issue under discussion is not an ethical one: Do humans have the right to use turtles for their own purposes—to kill them, eat their flesh and eggs, and turn their skin and shells into clothing and various decorative items? That's a legitimate, but separate, question. Rather, the issue is: What constitutes rational use, and what constitutes abuse? And further: Apart from use (and overuse), what other human actions pose the greatest threat to turtles? Which species are in the most danger? What are the consequences of exploitation, and what efforts are being made to save turtles from being exploited?

TURTLES AS FOOD

More than any other reptile, the turtle has been used by humans for food, and archaeological excavations indicate that this has been true for at least 20,000 years. Today, the turtle is unknown as food—or is consumed as a luxury or a novelty—in much of the Western world, but in many pre-industrial societies, turtle meat and eggs are staples and important sources of protein.

Marine and river turtles are eaten worldwide; they are hunted with bows and arrows, spears, harpoons, and nets. Tortoises, too, are taken universally for food; as Peter Pritchard points out, they "have a unique, and for them, disastrous combination of characteristics; they are . . . excellent to eat, ridiculously easy to catch, and with virtually no way of defending themselves."

In third world countries, people usually take only enough turtles and eggs to meet their immediate needs; their harvesting generally has not negatively affected local turtle populations on a long-term basis. For many of these people, the object of turtle hunting is survival. Or, as Fritz Obst succinctly puts it in *Turtles, Tortoises and Terrapins*: " . . . it is not the utilization of the creatures by primitive races that leads to their extinction, but the immoderate intervention of profit-seeking 'civilized' nations into the life and nature of tropical countries and their peoples."

For example, in the mid-nineteenth century, a European explorer, Walter Henry Bates, spent eleven years in the Amazon River basin; his book, *The Naturalist on the River Amazons*, published in 1863, describes how settlers and natives hunted turtles. Turtles (particularly the arrau river turtle) were killed for their meat, and their eggs were taken for oil, which was used for cooking and lighting; this practice had been carried on by the natives for hundreds of years.

With the coming of settlers from Europe, who persuaded natives to collect oil to sell for profit, the situation changed as the demand for oil skyrocketed. Based on the number of containers of oil collected in a year, and knowing how many eggs were needed to supply the contents of one container, Bates estimated that the total number of eggs destroyed amounted to 48 million in a single year.

© Dr. E.R. Degginger

Above: The remains of poached green turtles, found at the Sea of Cortez, Baja California.
Right: A sea turtle slaughterhouse, Costa Rica.

A false map turtle hatching.

Excessive egg-collecting in the Amazon continued to the extent that in this century the arrau turtle became a critically endangered species. And of course, the destruction of the giant tortoises of the Galapagos Islands and the islands off Madagascar provide another extreme illustration of Obst's statement.

Today, the turtles whose existence has been most threatened by the demand for their meat, skin, and shells are the big marine turtles. An account of their treatment serves to illustrate what is happening, in less dramatic ways, to other species of turtles all over the world because it results from the same shortsightedness and disregard.

The most frequently killed marine turtle, though not the most endangered (that dubious honor belongs to the Kemp's ridley) is the green turtle. Exploitation of the green turtle began in the mid-1600s, when the British colony at Jamaica sent ships to the Cayman Islands in the West Indies—considered by some to be the largest green turtle breeding grounds that have ever existed—to bring back turtle meat to feed the colony. By 1688, ships were carrying 13,000 turtles a year to Jamaica, and green turtle meat became the most frequently eaten meat there.

Laws prohibiting the collection of turtle eggs on any island belonging to Jamaica were enacted (but apparently not enforced) in the early 1700s. By the late 1700s, only a few turtles nested in the Caymans, and by 1840 ships were forced to travel all the way to the Miskito Cays off Nicaragua to obtain green turtles. By 1900, the nesting population in the Cayman Islands had been completely wiped out.

A brief history of the Miskito people of the eastern coast of Nicaragua, who hunt the green turtle, provides an excellent illustration of the ways which, in the modern world, economic and environmental concerns can become entangled to threaten both a human community and a species' existence.

For hundreds of years, the Miskito hunted the green turtle from open boats with harpoons; they became known as the best turtle hunters of the Caribbean. When they returned with the catch, the hunters shared turtle meat with the community in a ritual ceremony. In addition to turtle hunting, the Miskito provided for themselves by hunting and subsistence farming.

When Europeans came to Central America, they needed meat and were willing to pay the Miskito for it, first with goods, later with money. As agriculture, mining, and logging developed in Nicaragua, there was likewise an increasing demand for turtle meat, which the Miskito, abandoning their other economic activities, provided.

In short, the Miskito became dependent on, and victims of, a cash economy. As other industries shut down, their situation became more desperate; they were forced to spend more time hunting for turtles. In the 1960s, foreign concerns "helped" the Miskito by setting up turtle-processing plants and providing company boats and nets to increase the take of turtles.

The result is that the green turtle has become increasingly scarce as the Miskito have become more dependent on it for their livelihood. The social bonding produced by the ceremonial distribution of turtle flesh has been destroyed, and the Miskito now must sell turtles for

cash to buy food: flour, rice, beans, sugar, and coffee. And when the turtles become so scarce that it no longer makes economic sense to hunt them, what will the Miskito do? In this scenario, both the Miskito and the green turtle have become losers.

The wasted remains of a slaughtered sea turtle, probably poached.

Overhunting has affected other species as well. Once the arribadas of the Kemp's ridley at Tamaulipas became well known in the early 1960s, there was a wholesale slaughter of adults and collecting of eggs for almost half a decade. Finally, the Mexican government took measures to protect the turtles from poachers by using soldiers armed with submachine guns to patrol beaches.

As an indication of how thorough the plundering was, for a few years pack trains of forty to fifty burros were used to haul the eggs away, and from the 40,000 females that nested in the early 1960s, the numbers dwindled to about 4,000 turtles in the 1970s; today, only about 400 females remain. "Even with twenty years of good beach protection the species is declining, disappearing off the face of the Earth," Archie Carr said in an interview in the late 1980s.

The arribadas of the olive ridley at Escobilla Beach, Oaxaca, on the southwestern shore of Mexico, too, have been heavily raided. Hundreds of thousands of turtles have been killed there in the 1980s, and the number of nesting females has been reduced from a high of nearly 100,000 per year in 1968 to about 20,000 in the mid-1980s. The Mexican government has made a dedicated effort to protect both turtles and their nests against poachers by levying quotas and patrol-

A loggerhead lays her eggs near the Great
Barrier Reef in Australia.

© Gerry Ellis/Ellis Wildlife Collection

ing beaches, but the coastline is long and the resources for enforce-
ment sometimes have been scarce.

Another consequence of killing too many turtles and taking too
many eggs is that the maximum size of individual specimens has
declined. At the beginning of the twentieth century it was not unusual
to catch green turtles approaching a half-ton in size, but presently
300-pound (112-kilogram) specimens are considered unusually large.

Compared to the wholesale slaughter of sea turtles, the killing of
turtles for food by North Americans and Europeans has had a less
significant impact on turtle populations, though it has not been
inconsiderable. At different times in the past century, the diamondback terrapin population has been variously threatened, and alligator
snappers have become scarcer as well.

DEMAND FOR TORTOISESHELL AND TURTLE SKIN

Worldwide trade in commercial sea turtle products has increased
continuously throughout this century. A recent public television
special, *Sea Turtles: Ancient Nomads,* stated that there is more profit
to be made from sea turtle products than any other category of
animal on earth, and as a result, several turtle species are nearly
extinct.

The most affected species are the hawksbill (for the layered scutes
on its carapace, from which tortoiseshell is made) and the olive ridley
(for its skin, from which turtle leather is made). To a lesser extent, the
green turtle is also killed for tortoiseshell. Tortoiseshell and turtle-
leather products include bracelets, decorative combs, inlays, belts,
shoes, and handbags.

Three of the nations most heavily involved in producing products
made from turtle shells and skin are Japan, Mexico, and Indonesia.
According to Michael Weber, vice president of the Center for Marine
Conservation, Japanese trade in sea turtle products has cost the lives
of two million sea turtles since 1970. (One hawksbill yields up to
twelve pounds [four kilograms] of tortoiseshell.)

In 1980, according to one estimate, raw tortoiseshell was selling
for $45 a pound in Japan, and 45,000 pounds were being imported
annually for that country's crafts industry. Other sources estimate the

amount imported annually into Japan at closer to 100,000 pounds, up from 14,000 pounds per year in the early 1960s.

For many Japanese, turtles are a symbol of luck and prosperity, which explains the attraction of tortoiseshell products. It is said, for example, that a Japanese bride who doesn't have a tortoiseshell comb in her hair when she marries is bound to have misfortune. The annual use by the Japanese of nearly 9,000 lacquered, stuffed juvenile hawksbills as wall decorations already has been noted. In the mid-1980s, Indonesia was sending 28,000 hawksbills annually to Japan for processing.

Mexico and Ecuador harvested some 150,000 olive ridleys in 1979, primarily for their skins. This is an additional sad fact of "turtle economics"; frequently, the skin is what is considered valuable (only the flippers and skin of the neck is used) and turtle hunters throw the rest of the turtle overboard or leave it to rot on the beach.

Meanwhile, the turtle continues to become more scarce. The people of Indonesia, like the Miskito, have become entangled in the web of a cash economy. Efforts at conservation have been largely for naught; for those who hunt the hawksbill, it is often the best work they can find in areas where high unemployment is chronic.

Those who benefit most from the tortoiseshell and turtleskin trade are the wholesalers, and for them considerations of greed far outweigh any concern for the welfare of the turtles. Their attitude is that they will take all they can now, and when this resource is exhausted, they will turn to something else. "The trade in sea turtles is well-documented and grim," said Michael Weber. "Indonesia could take preventive measures, but it is shipping off its future to Japan."

The irony of the trade in tortoiseshell and turtle skin, of course, is that they are used entirely to make luxury products, and in every instance substitutes, many appearing almost identical to the genuine item, are available.

© David Niles

Dr. Peter Pritchard, one of the world's leading authorities on turtles, measures a leatherback.

Every year, 45,000 turtles, mostly loggerheads, are caught as "by-catch," along with tons of unwanted fish, in the nets of the 10,000 to 15,000 shrimp trawlers operating in the ocean waters off the southeastern United States. For every pound of shrimp obtained, ten pounds of fish and other bycatch are netted.

Because nets sometimes are dragged for hours before they are brought up, one in four trapped turtles drowns—more than 11,000 loggerheads annually, the largest single source of loggerhead mortality in the United States.

Trawlers also account for the deaths of about 750 Kemp's ridleys per year. "Far and away the most direct and injurious [threat against the Kemp's ridley] is the take by shrimp trawlers," Archie Carr said in the mid-1980s.

Fortunately, there is a simple, inexpensive solution to this problem. Developed over the past dozen years, it's known as the turtle excluder device—TED, for short. When attached to shrimp nets, TEDs allow turtles and up to 70 percent of the unwanted fish bycatch to pass through while still trapping shrimp, according to the U.S. Fish and Wildlife Service.

DEATH IN SHRIMPERS' NETS

Though even accidental killing of an endangered species is against the law, shrimpers have steadfastly resisted the use of TEDs, claiming that they let up to one-third of the shrimp pass through the nets. Although TEDs are inexpensive ($250–$400) and funds have been made available to purchase them, shrimpers consider them a nuisance. In 1987, less than 1 percent of the shrimp boats in operation employed TEDs.

"If TEDs aren't used, the Kemp's ridley will disappear within ten years," said Archie Carr. Apparently, the United States government agreed: Legislation was passed that required all commercial shrimp trawlers to use TEDs by mid-1989. In South Carolina, during the first two weeks of July 1989, turtle deaths were down dramatically after TEDs were put into use: Only six turtles were drowned, compared with an average of fifty-six during the same period over the previous nine years.

Shrimpers protested the regulations, however, blockading ports in Texas and Louisiana. This caused Commerce Secretary Robert Mosbacher to accede to the demands of shrimpers and politicians: On July 24 he suspended the regulations requiring the use of TEDs for forty-five days, ignoring the advice of scientific experts and Department of Commerce lawyers in the process. Politicians from Texas and Louisiana had argued that utilizing the TEDs was "shortsighted" and "would close out the livelihood of thousands of shrimpers."

Mosbacher proposed an alternative: hauling up the shrimp nets every 105 minutes in order to release any turtles caught during that time, despite evidence from the Coast Guard that almost all shrimpers were ignoring the rule.

Reaction from environmental groups was immediate and uncompromising. The National Wildlife Federation filed suit seeking a restraining order against Mosbacher's proposal, and on September 5, 1989, Mosbacher reversed his position, stating that the TEDs must be implemented. "This is a final decision on our part," spokesman Brian Gorman of the Commerce Department said.

DESTRUCTION AND OVERDEVELOPMENT OF NESTING GROUNDS

Turtles tend to nest on very expensive pieces of real estate. The loggerhead provides an excellent case in point. The largest loggerhead nesting grounds in the western Atlantic are on the beaches of six counties on the east coast of Florida; female loggerheads make about 10,000 nests there annually.

The problem is that these nests are very close to resorts and other centers of human population, and when the loggerhead hatchlings emerge, they often mistake the lights from inland for the ocean. Many head in the wrong direction, to be captured by predators, die from exposure to the sun, or be smashed by cars as they scurry across roads.

In other ways, in other places, the same scenario occurs wherever people settle undeveloped land. To mention only a few examples in the United States: Backhoes and dredging cranes alter the course of rivers and streams in a Louisiana backwater, disrupting the nests of snapping turtles; rangeland is expanded in the deserts of southeastern California, and the gopher tortoise suddenly must share its territory

Opposite page: A snapper confronts the handiwork of man—field fencing.

with cattle, sheep, and four-wheel-drive vehicles; the marshlands in the northeastern United States inhabited by the bog turtle continue to be drained and reclaimed.

ENVIRONMENTAL POLLUTION

Turtles undoubtedly suffer the short- and long-term effects of environmental pollution, especially in developed countries. As is the case with overdevelopment and disruption of their nesting sites, pollution is an "invisible" threat in that it is pervasive, low-profile (compared, say, to turtles being caught in shrimpers' nets), and to some degree simply taken for granted as a necessary accompaniment of population growth, movement, and industrialization.

The pollution of rivers, streams, and oceans with industrial byproducts has driven untold thousands of aquatic turtles from their homes and nesting places and killed untold thousands more. Undoubtedly, many turtles and tortoises have been killed by the effects of herbicides and insecticides in the food they eat and the air they breathe. The poisons no doubt accumulate in the turtles' fat, though it is difficult at present to document the long-term and/or genetic effects of their exposure to pollutants and pesticides.

We know at least two examples of turtle species that are harmed by our careless treatment of the environment. Many giant leatherbacks die because they mistake plastic bags floating in the ocean for their favorite food, jellyfish, and in eating them fatally clog their digestive tracts.

Perhaps worse is the fate of the many hatchlings who seek out floating islands of seaweed, kelp, and sargassum in which to spend the first few years of their lives. Unfortunately, these sources of nourishment and camouflage also are places where oil, styrofoam, and tar collect. Baby turtles often die from ingesting these materials. Even if the hatchlings don't eat them, the oil and tar produce sores and lesions on the turtles' skins, which can lead to infection.

EFFORTS AT TURTLE CONSERVATION AND PROTECTION

The most successful attempts at conserving and protecting turtles—the only concerted efforts, actually—have occurred during the past forty years. (By "conservation," that is "regulating the use of," by establishing quotas on the numbers of turtles that can be killed, for example. "Protection," on the other hand, means "preventing an animal, or its eggs, from being destroyed.")

Measures of conservation and protection have taken basically two forms: government legislation and action by individuals and organized groups. An element essential to their success is the agreement and cooperation of the people most affected by the policies.

One obstacle to the effectiveness of modern conservation and protection efforts is that they are almost always complicated, requiring the cooperation of several interest groups or nations.

In general, conservation and protection measures are necessary only when the intentional or incidental killing of turtles reaches widespread proportions, which almost always takes place only when turtles are the victims of commercial processing.

Discussing threats to the green turtle in 1975, Archie Carr said, "More than anything, the commercialization of turtle meat and

Upper left and upper right: Zoologists take a snapper's temperature and measurements, Great Swamp, New Jersey. *Above:* A turtle is transported from its breeding ground, while another is inspected *(right).*

Green turtle hatchlings in Grand Cayman.

© Phil Degginger

products has pushed the species to the brink of extinction. It isn't the Indians eating a few turtles on the beach for subsistence. It isn't the coastal people sharing meat among themselves that's the problem, it's that mass marketing that's going on in world trade that is."

Why would someone resist measures of conservation and protection? Sometimes, people's livelihoods are at stake: those of the United States shrimpers, for instance. As Peter Pritchard says, "The desirability of conservation of a natural resource is obvious to anyone who is able to think beyond his immediate needs . . . [and] if it doesn't require any sacrifice. The desirability of protection is less widely recognized since its benefits are less concrete. In many cases, protection involves a definite inconvenience to people, or restriction of their activities, and may cost a lot of money."

Sometimes people's lives are at stake, and the choices that must be made are not easy. In his wonderful personal narrative, *Time of the Turtle,* Jack Rudloe recounts a trip to Haiti to find a live hawksbill for the Philadelphia Zoo. There, at the Baptist Mission near Port-au-Prince, he saw hawksbill shells and tortoiseshell items for sale and asked a missionary if she wasn't aware that, next to the Kemp's ridley, hawskbills were the most threatened of the sea turtles.

The missionary replied: "'I know that hawksbills are becoming extinct. But they're going to become extinct regardless of what we do. A big shell like that sells for two hundred dollars. Do you know how much *food* that can buy for these people?'"

Rudloe took a good look at the people of Haiti: "I looked about the streets outside the mission. I looked at the children with their bones almost protruding through their rib cages. . . . Everywhere we went in Haiti, we were surrounded by a sea of beggars. . . . The missionaries told us how in times of drought and famine parents would look over their children and decide which ones shouldn't be given any food and allowed to starve to death so the rest could live. . .

"I didn't have the answers. How do you preach conservation to people who are starving, and are struggling to survive on an hour-by-hour basis? Yet, if something isn't done, the hawksbill and every other creature will disappear, and these people will still starve in the end."

LEGISLATION

Nevertheless, choices have to be made, especially where large-scale commercial processing of turtles is concerned. Legislation has made possible protective options that were once inconceivable when the most powerful economic group in an area was simply allowed to do as it pleased with turtles.

On an international basis, for example, the Convention on International Trade in Endangered Species (CITES) created a treaty in 1979 prohibiting trade in turtle products made from endangered species. The United States signed the treaty, but unfortunately not all nations have.

Also, all seven species of marine turtles have been classed as Endangered or Vulnerable in the International Union for the Conservation of Nature (IUCN) *Red Data Book of Amphibians and Rep-*

tiles. This document has been instrumental in encouraging countries all over the world to compile lists of endangered species and pass laws to protect them.

In the United States, all marine turtles except the Australian flatback are listed with the United States Fish and Wildlife Service, and as such receive protection as Threatened or Endangered species under the Endangered Species Act (50 CFR 17.11). Several other species of turtles, such as the diamondback terrapin, are given federal protection.

Some individual states have undertaken projects involving sea turtles. For example, in the late 1970s, North Carolina began a sea turtle nesting surveillance program to determine the distribution and density of sea turtle nesting activity throughout the state; this was later supplemented by the North Carolina Sea Turtle Stranding Network and other programs.

In addition, most states have laws protecting tortoises from injury, harrassment, or even from being taken as pets. In a recent ruling (summer 1989), the U.S. Fish and Wildlife Service, alarmed by a sudden decline in the desert tortoise population, responded to an emergency request by environmental groups and gave protection to the California desert tortoise, the official state reptile, as an endangered species. In late 1989, off-road motorcycle races were prohibited in certain sections of the southern California desert because of the threat to the well-being of the desert tortoise.

Government action in behalf of turtles has been initiated in other countries, as well. In the 1970s, the governments of Surinam, South

Hope for future generations. Conservation for slow-moving creatures *(above)*; raising green turtles at Grand Cayman *(below)*.

EFFORTS OF INDIVIDUALS AND INDEPENDENT ORGANIZATIONS

America, and Queensland, Australia, made it illegal to kill turtles or dig up their eggs. In both cases, the governments were persuaded by the actions of one or two crusading individuals.

If a single person could be said to symbolize individuals and independent organizations committed to turtle conservation and protection, it would be the late Archie Carr, who died in 1987 at the age of 77.

Carr was interested in reptiles—particularly turtles—all his life. He became a professor of biology at the University of Florida in the late 1930s, and was an author, lecturer, researcher, and expert on the sea turtles, especially the green turtle.

In 1955, Carr became involved, in his words, "in a campaign to rehabilitate the green turtle in the Caribbean Sea," in part as a source of food for native peoples. He was able to get research grants from the National Science Foundation and the Office of Naval Research to study the migrations of the green turtle.

Carr began at Tortuguero Beach, Costa Rica, then the only remaining nesting beach for the green turtle in the western Caribbean, at first working to protect the nesting areas from egg poachers. In 1957, the government closed the beach to exploitation.

In conjunction with the Caribbean Conservation Corporation, which he helped found, Carr began a turtle-tagging program at Tortuguero Research Station in order to study turtle-migration patterns. In three decades, Carr and those who followed him tagged nearly 30,000 turtles.

In "Operation Green Turtle," Carr and his associates attempted to re-establish breeding colonies of green turtles in places they once had been. The CCC did this by taking thousands of eggs or hatchlings from Tortuguero to other sites, such as Florida, the Bahamas, and other locations in the Caribbean, for reintroduction to the ocean.

The late Archie Carr and a green turtle crawling back to the water after burying her eggs. Carr spent most of his life studying turtles and working to protect the green turtle.

Archie Carr's conservation efforts over a period of thirty years not only saved the green turtle in the western Caribbean from destruction, it inspired others—largely local people, government officials, and university students—to follow his example in other areas as well, such as at Escobilla Beach in Oaxaca, the principal nesting site of the olive ridley. There, Mexican university students volunteer to tag and count hatchlings emerging from the sand.

Basically, all successful attempts to conserve and protect turtles—whether at the governmental or independent level—will require the elements Archie Carr brought to the endeavor: intelligence, knowledge, passion, purpose, perspective, and the capacity to inspire others to share a vision of what might be and to act on that vision.

Other organizations promoting conservation and protection of turtles (and other animals) include the World Wildlife Fund, the Natural Resources Defense Council, the Environmental Defense Fund, the Defenders of Wildlife, and the New York Zoological Society.

A green turtle swimming gracefully in the South Pacific.

To conclude this section of the book, I want to relate two cautionary tales. The first is a Cheyenne legend concerning the origins of a pit in the High Plains region of Oklahoma.

Long ago, the story goes, forty-nine men from the same warrior society, armed with stone-bladed axes and spears, set out on foot with their chief to hunt buffalo. They walked for many days without seeing any game; finally, they decided to return to camp, crossing a barren area known as the Staked Plains.

The men saw something bright shining in the distance, but paid it little heed, thinking it was a mirage. As they came closer, the object increased in brightness, reflecting the light of the sun. All morning they moved toward the shining object, and when they got close enough they saw that it was a huge water turtle, traveling at a steady pace toward the next water hole.

For a while, the men walked beside the huge turtle. Then, impulsively, one man jumped on its back; others followed suit, until finally all stood on top of the turtle's carapace, save the chief. He urged the men to climb down, exclaiming that the turtle was a powerful and mysterious force not to be taken lightly.

Some of the men poked at the turtle's shell with their spears, but others thought better of it and tried to descend to the ground. It was then that the men discovered they were stuck fast to the turtle and could not get off. Full of fear, they attacked the turtle's head and limbs, but their weapons only broke into pieces.

The men shouted to their chief to save them. He tried to reason with the turtle, exclaiming that if the turtle released the warriors, the tribe would honor it forever. The turtle took no notice of the chief's pleadings; instead, it kept moving steadily onward. Late in the day, the chief saw the turtle's destination: a large, flat, dark body of water. The warriors saw it, too, and they began to pray and cry out to the turtle for mercy. But the turtle merely walked on.

At last, the chief cried to the men trapped on the turtle's back. "I have done all I can do," he said. "You discovered something wonderful, but you did not respect it. Now you will be punished because of the evil in your hearts."

Then the turtle entered the lake. The men on the turtle's back watched their chief at the water's edge and waved to him. Slowly they sank, as the turtle walked into deeper water. The water rose to their waists, to their chests, and finally flowed over their heads and waving arms. Then the turtle and the men disappeared entirely, and all was still. Shaken, the chief returned home alone to tell the terrible news to his people.

The second story comes from a chapter in Jack Rudloe's *Time of the Turtle,* describing an experience Rudloe had as a young man aboard a shrimp trawler that incidentally had caught a male and female loggerhead in its nets. Touched by their plight, Rudloe suggested to a deckhand that he let the turtles go. At the time, loggerheads could be sold at the dock, and the deckhand refused. Rudloe even offered to pay the going price. The deckhand, annoyed that the turtles had shredded his nets with their beaks, still refused.

Malagasy men closely watch the movements of a radiated tortoise. The bond between man and other creatures on the planet is tenuous, at best.

For a day, Rudloe watched the two turtles writhe helplessly on the ship's deck. When the ship docked, the time came to butcher the turtles. Rudloe silently watched the process—which he describes in grim and gory detail—filled with a mixture of fascination and repulsion.

"I really had mixed feelings about the shrimpers," he says. "They had been my friends, let me go out on their boats, and given me more practical experience in marine biology than I could have learned in five years spent in a classroom. Shrimpers were among the last . . . free men in our society. Yet by killing sea turtles, they were doing a bad thing. They were pushing an already overexploited species to the verge of extinction."

The crewman who had butchered the two turtles, noting Rudloe's despair, handed him a mass of eggs from inside the female. "'I know what you're thinking, Jack,' he said defensively. 'Well, I'll tell you this, and Preacher will back it up. There's millions of turtles out there, and this little bit that these boats catch don't amount to nothing. The fish eat their babies or the birds get 'em. You could kill a thousand turtles, ten thousand turtles, and it wouldn't hurt!'"

Previously, it has been stated that it may seem that we hold all the cards in our relations with turtles; the truth, however, is that turtles have a power over us which all subordinate beings hold: the power—based on our actions—to reveal who we really are, our regard for the planet, and (since we have the capacity to destroy the Earth) our prospects for survival.

The stories I have just recounted—one a legend, the other factual—illustrate this truth and provide the same lessons: The only way for an individual, a group, or the human race to live responsibly is to experience ourselves as a part of the planet and its creatures rather than as separate beings, and to act in awareness of a larger reality rather than focusing only on narrow, short-term needs.

The Cheyenne warriors, for instance, treated the giant turtle as something alien, learning too late that their fate and the turtle's were one and the same. Further, the warriors' deaths resulted from who they were and what they chose, and past a certain point their fate was inevitable—there was no going back, no chance to make different choices.

Similarly, the turtle butcher created a narrow picture of reality based on his own needs rather than the facts ("You could kill . . . ten thousand turtles, and it wouldn't hurt!"). Had he been able to see beyond himself and acknowledge the precariousness of the loggerhead's existence, he might have released the animals instead of killing them.

Both stories presuppose an unstated condition: To learn anything of value from what turtles are trying to tell to us, we must first be listening. Are we? Some people, the Archie Carrs of the world, are. Others, the shrimpers who refuse to use TEDs, for instance, still have a distorted view of nature and the place of human beings in it.

That view, molded by greed and fear, could be summarized as follows: "Nature is there to be used as we see fit. Turtles stand between us and the shrimp. If we don't get the shrimp (each crew says), someone else will. Turtles are a nuisance, an inconvenience—they have to be sacrificed. Too bad, but that's the way it is." How else is it possible to explain the views of Southern congressmen who, speaking in behalf of the shrimpers, said that protecting a nearly extinct species is "shortsighted" and that relaxing the rules requiring the use of TEDs was "morally the right thing to do"?

Any fragile, integrated system can only stand so much abuse before it breaks down—in small, imperceptible ways or large, catastrophic ones. When turtles disappear in large numbers—through excessive killing, environmental poisoning, or simple neglect—it should serve as a warning that our lives and that of the planet are somehow out of balance, in ways that may be difficult or impossible to remedy.

In pre-industrial times, many Native Americans who lived by hunting and subsistence farming took the view that animals are too intelligent and powerful to fall prey to a hunter, but that animals understand that people need to eat, and so they sacrifice themselves from a sense of compassion. But for this arrangement to continue, human beings must have respect for animals and take only what they need; greed will be punished by the spirits.

In my view, we will have to begin to experience life in this way if we are to save the lives of turtles, other endangered species, and the planet. We will have to relinquish a certain power and arrogance that is deeply ingrained in industrial society.

Given that the lives of all creatures on the planet are inevitably and inextricably tied to one another, what will it take to survive? Resolute people who will put kindness and humanity in place of material progress. The absence of greed. Respect for nature and truth.

It is uncertain if such a transformation can take place, but we must act as if it can. We must make the viewpoint expressed in an old Pennsylvania Dutch proverb our own: We do not inherit the Earth from our ancestors; we borrow it from our children. Otherwise, in Archie Carr's words: "What we keep of the old earth will not be enough to save our honor with our descendants."

What will be its fate? A loggerhead reenters the surf after depositing her eggs.

CHAPTER FOUR

TURTLE CARE AND BREEDING

The information in this chapter is based upon material provided by Professor S. Frank, Dr. H. Schmidt, Mr. D. Reid, Mr. A. Wright, Mr. P. Green and Mr. G. Muller. We have tried to cover the care and breeding of the most commonly kept turtles, in some instances providing a number of alternatives for their successful maintenance. As with fish, there is more than one way to keep most reptiles, including turtles. Your local reptile society or pet store will be able to offer you useful advice, particularly with reference to local climatic conditions (where relevant). Turtles are "cold-blooded" (or, more correctly, "ecto-thermic"), that is, their body temperature is closely related to environmental temperatures. This is why many temperate species hibernate in the winter.

Experts now agree that the days of the dreadful "turtle bowl" are over. Steady warm temperatures, varied diet, and tank cleanliness are all vital for successful turtle raising.

Much has been said about the threats posed by turtles in spreading certain bacteria that are responsible for stomach upsets in humans. While it is true that turtles can carry these organisms, the likelihood of humans becoming infected can be all but eliminated by sensible personal and tank hygiene.

A tank for keeping fish is usually referred to as an aquarium, while a tank for turtles is referred to as a vivarium or aqua-terrarium, depending on the nature of the setup. Some species of turtle can also be kept in outdoor enclosures.

Armed with this information, you should be able to successfully care for the easily available turtles in your home or garden, and even breed them or perhaps specialize in some of the more unusual species. Do not forget to record your observations, carefully noting successes and failures; by doing so, you may well add to the store of knowledge of these interesting, popular, yet little-studied reptiles.

CARING FOR YOUR YOUNG TURTLE

To begin with, let us consider the care of young hatchling turtles, such as the sliders, red-ears, and map turtles (*Pseudemys, Chrysemys, Graptemys*). You will need an aquarium with a suitable island of smooth rocks or floating cork. The minimum size of the aquarium should be 24 by 12 by 12 inches (60 by 30 by 30 centimeters), for even young turtles must be given a large area for swimming. Even in a tank of this size, however, you should not try to keep more than two or three hatchlings. A water depth of 6 to 10 inches (15 to 25 centimeters) is advised. In most literature it is recommended that the water level for baby turtles not be deeper than the length of the animal's shell. With water at this level, the baby turtle will be able to obtain air readily by standing on its hind legs and stretching above the surface of the water.

Such conditions do not, however, fit in either with these animals' natural habitat or with observations based on experience. When danger threatens in the wild, the hatchling sets off in a beeline to the nearest pond and throws itself into the water. Even the smallest of these pools always has a greater depth of water than the "puddles" that are generally recommended. A water level of 12 to 15 inches (30 to 37.5 centimeters) is the minimum depth that one would expect to find in a natural pond or lake. Banks of a pond frequently have steep slopes, and it is precisely these spots that the turtles prefer because, when threatened, they can dive quickly into deep water and so make their escape. Shallow water, in contrast, does not present any problems for potential predators and so does not afford any protection for the turtle.

While it is true that the hatchling has to scramble about rather frantically in the deeper water in order to get to the surface for air, and that it expends a lot of energy in doing so, this action increases its appetite, and the increased food intake promotes muscle formation and greatly benefits the animal's circulation.

Our own experience leads us to suggest that hatchlings should be put into an aquarium at least 12 inches wide and 24 to 30 inches (60 to 75 centimeters) long, with a water depth of about 8 inches (20 centimeters), immediately after hatching. The behavior of the young turtles seems to confirm this repeatedly and consistently. A healthy youngster will feel the need to come up for air after about a minute. It starts to tread water and usually makes its way to the surface quite quickly. The baby turtle often learns from this very first attempt—at most after three attempts—how to turn its frantic swimming technique into a smooth gliding motion. The initial, frenzied flailing around with its legs are soon replaced by calm swimming strokes. On the basis of this initial behavior one can quickly determine whether or not a hatchling is healthy, for only healthy specimens react in the manner described above. If one is considering buying young stock, care should be taken to ensure that specimens offered for sale are displaying the calm, coordinated mode of swimming, because the difficulties associated with the initial contact with water should already have been overcome. Only alert, active, feeding turtles should be selected; those with cloudy or swollen eyes, or runny noses and troubled breathing, should be avoided.

In order to help keep the aquarium clean, it is best to do without loose bottom material. To achieve an attractive effect, fine gravel or sand and larger pebbles can be stuck to the bottom with aquarium sealer. If this is done, care must be taken to make sure that the tank is left filled with water for several days and refilled with fresh water before the turtles are placed in it, in order to ensure that any poisonous elements of the sealer that may have dissolved into the water have been flushed away.

The cork island or smooth rocks are very important, as the small turtles must be able to climb easily out of the water—and without damaging their lower shell. The island must therefore slope gently into the water, with part of it completely dry. Food can be placed in the "shallows" around the island (and easily removed if uneaten).

In order to overcome the need for a daily water change—which, apart from the work involved, also generally means disturbing the animals—filtration is recommended. The filter requirements depend upon the size of tank and the number of animals who will live in it, but utmost care should always be taken to choose an *efficient* filter (small power filters or foam cartridge filters are ideal). Young turtles eat a lot of food and excrete a correspondingly large amount of waste. For this reason it is necessary to use a filter with a considerably higher capacity than that used for a tank of similar size that is occupied by fish. The type of filter media used for fish tanks, namely peat fiber, activated charcoal, and nylon wool, is not suitable for turtle tanks. The fiber material would be blocked with feces and bits of food in no time at all, and the flow of water would all but cease. A suitable type of medium for a turtle tank is foam, which is supplied with some cartridge filters and power filters, or, in the case of power filters, a layer of gravel or ceramic filter medium followed by a smaller layer of activated carbon. In either case, the filters will need regular washing or renewal of medium or media, the frequency of which can be gauged by the fall in filter output. Weekly to monthly servicing is generally the rule.

An attractively marked young red-eared slider, *Pseudemys* or *Chrysemys scripta elegans.*

© B. Kahl/Tetra

© B. Kahl/Tetra

Although small, the common red-eared slider has a powerful bite.

nately, the beneficial effects of natural sunlight are lost when light passes through glass, even if just a single layer.

To ensure that your turtles are never exposed to extreme or fluctuating temperatures, it is a good idea to mount a liquid crystal thermometer on the outside of the aqua-terrarium; this will allow you to obtain temperature readouts quickly and easily. Similarly, your turtles must always have access to a small area of shade. Hopefully the days of the awful "turtle bowl" are over, but the setup required for two or three hatchling red-ears need not be any more elaborate than that used for a community tank of tropical fishes.

Nonetheless, even with efficient filtration, the water in the turtle tank will have to be replaced every 7 to 14 days with fresh tap water at the correct temperature. Never expose young turtles to sudden changes in temperature, as they are very sensitive and "chill" very easily.

One easy method for keeping the water in the turtle tank at the required 77°F to 86°F (25°C to 30°C) is using a reliable aquarium heater-thermostat, taking care to ensure that the heater and thermostat are both covered with water at all times. A cover or hood, with suitable holes for ventilation, will keep the temperature of the air in the tank from falling too low during cool weather, and will also help to prevent drafts.

Young turtles especially seem to benefit from "sunbathing"—in either natural sunlight or artificial sunlight (as supplied by fluorescent tubes or low-wattage bulbs). Sunlight or above-tank artificial lights must never be allowed to overheat the tank, and very often a 25- or 40-watt tungsten light bulb (left on for a few hours a day) is quite adequate. Some herpetologists (that is, people specializing in the study of reptiles and amphibians) even use special fluorescent tubes or bulbs that are rich in light toward the ultraviolet (UV) end of the spectrum. It appears that as well as having worthwhile psychological effects on turtles, the UV light found in both natural, unfiltered sunlight and these special bulbs or tubes is important in helping the formation of vitamin D_3, which aids in bone formation. Unfortu-

FEEDING YOUR AQUATIC TURTLE

If turtles are to thrive in captivity, a varied diet is absolutely essential. This requirement is especially critical in young specimens. Many different kinds of "worms," such as tubificids (*Tubifex* sp.), enchytraeids (*Enchytraeus* sp.), and chopped earthworms (*Lumbricus* sp.), but not the intensely red-colored species of the genera *Eiseniella* and *Allolobophora*, among others; small crustacea like water fleas (*Daphnia* sp.); sand hoppers (*Gammarus* sp.); aquatic insect larvae like the wormlike representatives of the midges (*Chironomus* sp.); aquatic snails (*Lymnaea planorbis*); and many other water creatures that can be netted from natural ponds or even swilled off aquatic plants into a bucket of water are ideal food. If the water from such a bucket is poured through a sieve, the resulting yield of water creatures—worms, crustaceans, and insect larvae in abundance—will serve as a good source of food.

These creatures represent the most natural form of food for young turtles and one would be hard pressed to find a better substitute. If there are no ponds in your neighborhood then "meadow plankton" offers a good alternative. To obtain this, go for a walk in the fields during the warm months of the year, armed with a small-meshed net to drag lightly over the surface of the grass. You will soon have a rich harvest of insects and spiders that you can kill by dipping your net into hot water before you feed them to your pets. This will prevent the insects—many of which can fly—from escaping all over your house. If you cannot harvest foods from the wild in either of these ways, you can obtain commercially produced "turtle foods" from dealers. Some of these represent a balanced mixture of ingredients that ensures your animals a proper diet. This makes it possible for anyone to keep these creatures as pets, even if they do not have access to a source of natural food. Such ready-made foods are also suitable for adult specimens if they are given in larger amounts. Fine pellets will lead to rapid contamination of the water. Avoid the use of dried ant eggs and other dried foods of low nutritional value, and choose a high-quality prepared diet from a reliable manufacturer. Such prepared diets are obviously more convenient than live foods, and some variety can be provided by using tablet or pellet foods intended for fish or by using fresh foods.

Fresh foods can take the form of lean, finely scraped raw meat or raw fish, and finely chopped whole fish is an especially good food. Some soft vegetable matter, including lettuce and water weeds like *Egeria (Elodea),* should also be provided from time to time.

In an emergency, or to provide yet more variety, canned dog or cat food can also be used to feed turtles. Furthermore, you can even prepare your own complete "Turtle's Delight" diet as follows:

> 1 quart milk (1.5% fat is best)
> 5 eggs
> 2 pounds carrots (sliced and slightly boiled; retain water for mixing)
> ½ pound oat flakes
> 2 pounds cuttlefish (*Sepia* or *Octopus*)
> 2 pounds lean, whole freshwater fish
> 1 pound shrimp
> 1 pound ox liver
> Multivitamin mineral supplement suitable for turtles (seek advice of veterinarian)
> About 1 pound food gelatin
> 3 teaspoons sea algae flour
> 2 quarts water

In a mixer, reduce all the solid ingredients to a mash. Stir this in with the eggs, milk, and one quart of the water. Dissolve the gelatin mixture in the second quart of water at about 175°F (80°C); let it cool to about 120°F (50°C), then add to the food mash, which has since been heated to about 85°F to 105°F (30°C to 40°C). Finally, stir the sea algae flour and the multivitamin supplement into the mixture. This recipe will yield 7 to 8 quarts of high-grade turtle food. Packed into portions and quickly deep-frozen, this food can be stored in your household freezer. The supply will last for several weeks, depending on how many animals you have. Two to three hours of work are involved in the preparation. Young, growing turtles should be fed on a suitable diet, once a day, with as much as is consumed in a few minutes. Older turtles tend toward obesity, and should therefore be fed only two or three times a week. Since healthy turtles have a hearty appetite but are rather messy feeders, removal of the turtles to a special "feeding bowl" (containing water at the same temperature as their tanks) will help to keep their tank cleaner for longer.

CARING FOR YOUR ADULT TURTLE

With proper care and a good, varied diet, your young hatchling turtle can grow quite rapidly. This rate of growth is an important

A typical pet red-eared slider, *Pseudemys* or *Chrysemys scripta elegans.*

Tetra Archive

© B. Kahl/Tetra

A beautiful example of the species *Pseudemys floridana.*

factor that must be taken into account when purchasing a tank and deciding on how many hatchlings to start with.

For larger, adult turtles, their vivarium or aqua-terrarium must have a zone of water that amounts to at least 70% of the tank volume. A minimum water depth of 10 inches (25 centimeters) is required, though 20 to 24 inches (50 to 60 centimeters) is better. Although a banked landscape with a gently rising slope would be the ideal, this is only a realistic proposition outdoors or in very large tanks. In order to obtain the optimum level of utilizable space, and above all to leave a sufficiently large swimming area, the following tank arrangement is recommended.

A tank for more than one adult turtle should be at least three feet in length. The number of specimens to be kept and their eventual adult size will determine the dimensions of the tank. This aqua-terrarium should have a perforated cover or hood into which one or two low-wattage light bulbs can be placed. In very large tanks, mercury vapor (or similar) spotlights can be used, but watch out for overheating.

The water in this setup can be maintained at a steady 68°F to 77°F (20°C to 25°C) using an aquarium thermostat. If you are keeping large, robust turtles, the heater-thermostat should be protected within a coarse nylon-mesh cylinder (open at both ends). This will allow it to carry out its temperature-controlling functions, but prevent the turtle from damaging it.

Larger turtles obviously need a suitably sized and stable land area onto which they can climb completely out of the water. One way to achieve this is to divide the tank in two by inserting a vertical sheet of glass, which can be sealed in place using aquarium sealer. The area on one side of the divider can then be filled with water, that on the other with dry, coarse gravel. A gently sloping ramp will allow the turtle to leave the water and climb onto the gravel "bench." Any sharp edges must be avoided.

The aqua-terrarium should otherwise be quite bare, and should incorporate a reliable power filter (as discussed at the beginning of this chapter). Since sliders, red-ears, and their relatives are particularly fond of sunshine, it is possible to keep them out of doors during the warmer months of the year. Anyone who has a garden pond located in a sunny spot and can rule out the possibility of escape through the judicious use of a barrier should take advantage of this ideal type of quarters on a temporary basis. For some species, a period in the open is a prerequisite if they are to breed.

In cases where a new pond is being planned, a plastic or fiberglass preformed pool, or a pond made with a plastic liner are to be preferred to a concrete version. Leaks that occur over the years and are difficult to repair, as well as the poorer heat-retention properties, are disadvantages inherent to a concrete pond. In contrast, plastic or fiberglass ponds are largely unaffected by frost and heat, should maintain a stable shape, have an almost unlimited life, and are poor conductors of heat. Ponds made by placing a plastic liner over a pit dug in the ground can be designed and laid out at will, and are also very durable.

To eliminate any risk, a close-meshed metal grating (to protect against mice) should be laid in the pit after the soil has been excavated. In order to help the liner sit snugly on the earth base, first a layer of loam and then a covering of sand should be laid down. To ensure a long service life a high-quality liner that is resistant to sunlight is essential. It is often pointless to try to grow plants in company with any but the youngest turtles. With older specimens, the planted part can be made inaccessible. Further information on the outdoor care of turtles is provided below.

KEEPING TURTLES OUT!

Because of the mass movement of hatchling red-eared turtles or sliders through the pet trade and the improper care of these creatures, there is a high incidence of mortality. The following information should give would-be turtle-keepers the expertise to care responsibly for their charges. Although dealing briefly with their care in aquariums, emphasis is placed on the benefits of maintaining red-ears and other turtles in outdoor enclosures.

The red-eared turtle *Chrysemys* (or *Pseudemys*) *scripta elegans* is widespread over the southern and central United States, from Texas to Illinois and Indiana. Its range has been increased by escapes and by introduction into new areas.

A very aquatic reptile, the red-eared turtle prefers still or slow-moving water where it can forage and hide in dense aquatic vegetation. In the wild it is a shy creature and prefers to bask mainly on submerged logs, rather than coming onto dry land.

Young specimens have an attractive olive-green carapace (upper shell) and a yellow or cream plastron (lower shell) marked with a few black genetic markings. The limbs and head are green and cream-striped, and on each side of the neck is a red or orange flash that gives this turtle its common name. In adult specimens the green coloration turns to black or dark gray-brown, but the cream striping and red streak invariably remain. Males can be identified by their larger tails and by long claws on the forelimbs.

Turtles can thrive in captivity only if they are given adequate, clean accommodations and the correct diet. Not having the first of these is one of the reasons that so many baby turtles perish. Because of their size and construction, the little "turtle bowls" sold in pet shops are quite useless. An aquarium is far more suitable. There should be ample swimming space and a water depth of no less than the length of the largest specimen kept. The water should be heated to about 75°F (25°C) using a submersible heater-thermostat. A small land area will give the turtles an opportunity to lie under a lamp that offers a basking temperature of about 80°F (27°C). This lamp must be switched off at night.

Turtles invariably feed in the water, and this means that frequent cleaning of the tank is necessary. Because turtles are messy feeders, good power filtration will be needed to cope with the consequences. If possible, some form of drainage equipment should be fitted into the base of the tank to make cleaning easier; regular siphoning and scrubbing, however, is still unavoidable.

Although small red-eared turtles (and other species of turtle that can be kept in similar conditions) will survive indoors, older specimens can successfully thrive, grow, and even breed in an outdoor enclosure, or "reptiliary." A medium or large pond—minimum size is approximately 20 square feet—with a surrounding land area enclosed by a perimeter wall will house four to eight adult red-ears and, if conditions allow, can be shared with other reptiles and/or amphibians.

An outdoor reptiliary should be in a sunny position and must be well drained. Construction of the pond should be carried out before the perimeter is built. The pond lining can be made of concrete, fiberglass, or preformed plastic. Flexible pool liners, with the exception of butyl, are not usually strong enough to withstand the turtles' claws.

If the turtles are to hibernate in situ, the pond must be at least 24 inches (60 centimeters) deep. A shallower area planted with marginals will offer food, shelter, and security to the inhabitants. Aquatic vegetation planted in the deeper parts is certain to be eaten sooner or later, so it makes little sense to cultivate expensive specimen plants such as lilies. Fast-growing aquatics like *Egeria (Elodea) densa* and *Myriophyllum* are ideal, but be prepared to replace them periodically.

An old tree stump placed in the water and weighted with rocks until it becomes waterlogged will provide a basking platform similar to that which the turtles would favor in the wild. A well-shaped stump or log will also add an attractive feature to the setting.

If the pool is large and contains a variety of animal life—something that should be encouraged, to provide extra food for the turtles—frequent cleaning should be unnecessary. However, some provision for draining or pump-assisted siphoning is advisable.

The edge of the pond should have several ramps by which the turtles can enter and leave the water freely.

The surrounding land area may not be utilized very much by the turtles, but it still will serve several purposes. The distance between pond and perimeter wall will give a sense of security to the turtles because "intruders" rarely approach the pond closely. This area will also harbor natural plant and animal life, thereby further extending the turtles' feeding opportunities. And terrestrial reptiles and even a few amphibians can be kept in company with the turtles, making the reptiliary more interesting and varied.

Turtles living outdoors soon become very shy; that is, they come to behave "normally," as if they had been born in the wild, unlike those kept in vivaria. The feeling of security presented by the wall should therefore allow viewing without disturbing the creatures. A well laid-out covering of plant life—natural vegetation is preferred to cultivated, or "foreign," plants—will give shelter to other inmates and provide all the inhabitants with insects and other invertebrates as food. Old logs and rocks further add to the habitat. One or two small shrubs providing some shade may be beneficial in excessively sunny weather. These must be kept clear of the perimeter wall. Careful consideration must be given to the design of the wall; it not only has to retain the inmates, but must keep out unwanted visitors. A solid wall is therefore better than any form of wire mesh.

The wall, preferably built of brick, should be at least 24 inches (60 centimeters) high and surmounted by an overhang on both sides. If lizards are to be included in the reptiliary, a strip of laminated plastic or a row of plastic or ceramic tiles should be fixed around the inside of the wall near the top, as lizards can cling to most brick or cement surfaces no matter how smooth. Never lean branches or other potential bridges to freedom against the wall.

Excluding unwelcome creatures may pose more of a problem than keeping the rightful inhabitants in. The turtles will be shy enough to avoid the attentions of curious dogs and cats, but discouraging these large potential predators can be difficult without resorting to unsightly wire mesh coverings or similar drastic measures.

Rats and other small wild animals with predatory inclinations will be unable to scale a smooth vertical surface or to negotiate the external overhand on top of the wall; and if birds become a problem, a fine garden netting can be used to enclose part or all of the area.

In seasons of very wet weather the reptiliary could become flooded if the surrounding wall does not have a few drainage holes at the base. These must be covered with wire mesh to prevent small captives from escaping and to foil intruders. The holes must be kept clear of fallen leaves and other debris.

The diet of wild turtles consists of fish, crustaceans, insects, carrion, and aquatic vegetation. In captivity, their diet is subject to greater abuse than any other factor of their husbandry. It is still common practice in pet shops to sell tubs of dried mixtures, many of which are quite incapable of promoting healthy development, under the name "turtle food."

Although several food animals will find their way naturally into the reptiliary, others can be introduced. Water snails will reproduce freely in the pond, and if there is sufficient cover to establish themselves a continuous supply of nutritious food will be available.

Freshwater fish are unlikely to reproduce at a rate fast enough to make them an uninterrupted food source, but periodic introduction of a moderate quantity of small goldfish, minnows, and other very small fish will ensure the availability of valuable animal protein for the turtles.

Feeds of whole dead animals such as fish can be offered once or twice a week. A whole animal is essentially a "balanced" meal and a convenient way of supplying a nutritious diet, and most healthy captive turtles receive at least half of their food in this form. However, excellent compound foods for reptiles and amphibians have recently been developed by responsible animal food producers (e.g., ReptoMin, by Tetra).

Worms, insects, land snails, green vegetation, and liver (rich in vitamin A, a deficiency of which may lead to the familiar problem of swollen eyes) should occasionally be offered.

If the diet is sufficiently varied, vitamin-mineral supplementation should not be necessary. Catching reptiliary-kept turtles for administration of additives or corrective medication is far from easy, emphasizing the importance of adequate diet.

Outdoor living conditions offer the best chances for breeding turtles. Despite the vast numbers of turtles that have been bought by private owners, very few breedings have been recorded.

Because turtles, like most reptiles, bury their eggs, a few suitable sites should be prepared in the reptiliary. These areas should be well drained and in a sunny position, and in temperate climates, a slight south-facing slope is preferred.

Turtles are well able to dig into the ground using their powerful hind limbs, but a light forking over of the likely nest sites will make their excavations easier. Light-colored sand sprinkled over the areas will help the turtle-keeper to locate the eggs, as all chelonians (turtles, tortoises, and terrapins) leave little or no sign of ground disturbance when filling in is completed. The eggs are deposited about 4 to 6 inches (10 to 15 centimeters) below the surface.

Egg-laying usually takes place about five to six weeks after mating. However, this may

Chinemys reevesii, with its characteristically keeled carapace, is an Asian species that is less available now than it was a few years ago.

Tetra Archive

be extended, sometimes considerably. In fact, it has been recorded that female red-eared turtles practice sperm-retention, laying fertile eggs perhaps two or more years after insemination. Because it is unlikely that eggs will hatch successfully if left in the ground in temperate regions, they must be carefully removed for incubation.

Removed eggs should be half-buried in a covered plastic box containing slightly damp sand or vermiculite. Incubation temperature should be 85°F to 86°F (29°C to 30°C), with high humidity. Disturbance of the eggs must be minimal.

Hatching takes place beginning after about 54 days after laying, but again this may be extended, even to 150 days (dependent upon temperature). Hatchlings are approximately one inch in diameter. They require a variety of nutritious foods such as small fish, snails, and worms. A small piece of cuttlebone left in the water will help promote normal shell development.

For the first few months, it is advisable to house baby turtles in a tank kept at a temperature of about 75°F to 85°F (25°C to 30°C). However, they will benefit from being placed outdoors on warm days and brought in at night.

When low temperature precludes normal activity, turtles are obliged to hibernate. Many keepers find that the safest procedure in winter is to bring the turtles into heated accommodations, thus keeping them active throughout the year. This may contribute to the low birth rate in captivity, as a period of cooling, if not actual hibernation, seems conducive to breeding. If temperatures are consistently below about 55°F (13°C), the turtles are unlikely to feed. This will not be harmful if the cool starvation period is no longer than four to six weeks.

It is possible for healthy adult red-eared turtles to successfully hibernate in an outdoor pond through a particularly harsh winter, but this is inadvisable unless the physiology of hibernation is thoroughly understood. The hibernation period is spent buried in the debris at the bottom of the pond, below the depth at which the water is likely to freeze. In temperate climates, this may be 24 inches (60 centimeters) or more below the surface of the water. Turtles should not be subjected to sub-optimal temperatures until all digestion is completed. Therefore a starvation period of about 10 days prior to cooling is essential.

Because of the popularity of the red-eared turtle, we have focused on this species in our description of outdoor "housing." Other species may also be housed in the same conditions.

Other familiar examples include North American species such as painted turtles (*Chrysemys picta*); map and sawback turtles (*Graptemys* sp.); mud and musk turtles (*Kinosternon* and *Sternotherus* sp.); and the European genera *Emys* and *Mauremys*. The more terrestrial box turtles (*Terrapene* spp.) are also suitable for the outdoor reptiliary, as are the terrestrial *Gopherus, Geochelone,* and *Testudo.* However, these completely terrestrial species must be prevented from falling into the deep pond, and in the case of tropical or semitropical species, facilities will probably have to be provided to overwinter the chelonians in a suitable indoor enclosure. Some of the hardier species of lizard can also be kept in association with the turtles. Examples are the fence lizards *Sceloporus,* skinks *Eumeces,* and the European *Lacerta* and *Podarcis.* Frogs and toads are

An example of a rather elaborate aqua-terrarium.

© C. Andrews/Tetra

Tetra Archive

sometimes housed with turtles, but the risk of the aquatic amphibians becoming a meal for the voracious reptiles is considerable.

DID YOU KNOW...?

Provided below is a collection of miscellaneous information on chelonians.

1. There are over 5,000 species of reptiles alive in the world today, but only about 300 or so of these species are turtles, terrapins, or tortoises.
2. Turtles range in size from the familiar freshwater red-ears, sliders, and map turtles described in this chapter to the giant leatherback marine turtle (*Dermochelys*), which may weigh over 1,500 pounds and grow to 6 feet in length.
3. According to the *Guinness Book of Animal Facts and Feats,* the greatest authenticated age for a turtle is at least 152 years—for a Seychelles giant tortoise (*Geochelone*). Some authorities claim that this individual may have been at least 180 years old when it died in 1918. Even among more familiar species, records of 50 or 100 years of age are not uncommon.
4. Many of the commonly kept pet turtles are now bred on "turtle farms" as far afield as the Far East.
5. In France, turtle-keeping is more popular than fish-keeping.
6. As is common with many other animals, even healthy turtles may carry the *Salmonella* bacterium, which can cause stomach upset in humans. It is therefore important that you always wash your hands after handling your turtle and that you never discard water from the turtle tank into a sink used for washing or food preparation.
7. Fish, frogs, newts, and salamanders do not make good tank companions for turtles. Even tiny hatchlings can cause havoc in a planted aquarium and can be a little "snappy" toward slow-moving fish and amphibians.
8. The collection from the wild and trading of some aquatic turtles and land tortoises is now controlled by law in many countries, including Britain and North America. Would-be herpetologists should therefore deal only with reputable suppliers; if in doubt, information as to who is "reputable" can be obtained from the relevant local government conservation or wildlife office.

The Asian box turtle, *Cuora* spp., is more aquatic and less hardy than its North American namesake, *Terrapene.*

9. On land, turtles may appear to be slow-moving, lumbering individuals, but in water some marine species can swim at speeds of up to 20 miles per hour over short distances.

10. There are records of over-amorous but short-sighted male marine turtles attacking scuba divers. Fortunately, such events are fairly unusual.

And who said turtles were not interesting?

TORTOISE AND BOX TURTLE REVIVAL

It was perhaps coincidental that a total ban on the import of Mediterranean land tortoises into the United Kingdom should occur at a time when more interest than ever before was being shown in the tortoise as a pet animal. Previously, this animal was regarded as little more than a mobile garden ornament. Although serious enthusiasts had long appreciated the tortoise life-style, these creatures were invariably kept on an inadequate diet in sub-optimal conditions. Consequently, mortality was high.

The import ban will certainly not solve all the tortoises' problems, but the new awareness of their plight has fostered real advances in husbandry, particularly in breeding and the raising of the young.

The tortoise calendar begins in early spring. Having awakened from a hibernation that lasted throughout the winter months, the tortoise must replenish the store of energy that its body utilized while in the torpid state.

Hibernation is often completely misunderstood. Far from being a voluntary sleep in a warm den, it is a state of near-coma induced by low temperatures. The body goes into this state when its temperature drops to a point at which normal digestion and other functions are not possible. The metabolism of reptiles—and of other ectothermic creatures—is totally dependent on temperature. As the temperature approaches the freezing point, the metabolic rate slows correspondingly until, at around 32°F (0°C), metabolism stops and death results.

Conversely, as the temperature rises bodily functions operate progressively faster and

will need sustaining (i.e., feeding). The ideal hibernation temperature is therefore about 41°F to 46°F (5°C to 8°C). In the wild, hibernation may last for only a few weeks, but in captivity in temperate climates this may be extended to five or six months. To sustain itself for such a long period, the tortoise must be properly prepared. Diet plays a crucial part in this.

Tortoises are principally plant eaters, but they will often consume animals and insects. Captive herbivores present several problems. It is virtually impossible to accurately predict the tortoises' subtle requirements as found in the many and varied plant species that form the natural diet. And even if turtle-keepers could offer the same vegetation as that eaten in the wild, the nutritional value of these plants could be upset by the artificial growing conditions and storing methods used in their cultivation.

When free to roam in a large, planted enclosure, tortoises have a tremendous advantage over those restricted to small runs and subject to limited substitute diets. They can forage for the nourishment they require, rather than relying on an offered diet that will inevitably be deficient. For example, a recent paper on Hermann's tortoise (*Testudo hermanni*) in Yugoslavia remarks that among the principal foods were the plant families Leguminosae (33.3%) and Ranunculaceae (25%). It is extremely unlikely that plants from either of these families appear in significant amounts in prepared diets.

Lettuce, probably the food plant most often offered to captive tortoises, contains little nourishment and is certainly not a food item available to tortoises in the wild. Unfortunately, tortoises seem to develop a liking for lettuce to the exclusion of all else; as is true of children who would exist solely on sweets if given the chance, this predilection is not an indication of nutritional value. A large enclosure should be left to naturally develop its own growth of native plants in as great a variety as possible. It should not be difficult to propagate weeds. Low bushes and small trees offer shelter and shade, as well as additional foods in the shape of fallen fruit and leaves, which are avidly consumed in the fall.

If there is sufficient natural shelter it may be possible, even beneficial, to allow the tortoise to hibernate outdoors. The

Opposite page: A group of young turtles, including the map turtle *Graptemys kohnii* and the red-eared slider, *Pseudemys* or *Chrysemys scripta elegans.*

eighteenth-century English naturalist Gilbert White successfully maintained a spur-thighed tortoise (*Testudo graeca*) in this way for over 40 years in southern England. However, possible protracted periods of extremely low winter temperatures in more northerly latitudes must be considered as detrimental in most situations. In a natural enclosure the two main facets of tortoise husbandry are provided for; adequate diet will allow extended hibernation, and the cover offered by mature vegetation may ensure a satisfactory "hibernaculum," or hibernating area.

Because tortoises are surprisingly adept climbers, the enclosure's perimeter fence must be at least 15 inches high; if wire mesh is used, an overhang must also be fitted. Since they can also dig, the fence should extend some 8 inches below ground.

A shallow pond with easy access should be kept filled with clean water at all times, for tortoises may drink copiously. During hibernation there will have been some dehydration, so water usually takes priority over food on emergence.

If shade and shelter are not available in the form of natural vegetation, a hide box must be provided. This should be raised above the ground and roofed with a waterproof material to prevent it becoming damp, and it should be loosely packed with straw or dead leaves. The bedding should be changed regularly.

Given the correct basic conditions, tortoises will readily mate in captivity. Compe-

The seldomly kept diamondback turtle, *Malaclemys terrapin*, was once hunted almost to extinction in its North American home.

Tetra Archive

tition for females is quite intense as male tortoises are notably violent in their courtship. There is little or no male-male aggression, but the "softening up" of the females is a different matter. The courting male will repeatedly take savage bites at the female's limbs, occasionally drawing blood. He will also butt her, flinging himself forward with as much power as his limbs can muster and withdrawing his head just before contact is made. The clash of shell against shell reverberates around the tortoise enclosure during spring and summer.

Eventually, the female gives in to the persistently vigorous attentions and allows the male to mount her. His intermittent thrusts are accompanied by comical squeaks from his gaping mouth.

When six weeks have elapsed from the time of successful mating, the female may start looking for a suitable laying site. She will be seeking the correct conditions for incubation of the eggs. She may dig one or two trial nest holes before she finds a site that satisfies her.

As it is unlikely that the eggs will hatch in an unstable temperate climate if left in the ground, they must be carefully excavated for artificial incubation. Finding the eggs may prove difficult as the female effectively disguises her work. Sprinkling likely nesting areas with light-colored sand will help to identify the disturbed site.

For artificial incubation, the eggs should be placed in a plastic box half-filled with sterilized sand. The eggs need not be completely covered by the medium, which should be dry or slightly damp. The box should have a tight-fitting lid with one or two small air holes. Visual inspection of the eggs every two days will ensure that the air in the box does not become too stale.

The eggs should not be handled unnecessarily. It is commonly believed that tortoise eggs should never be turned during incubation, but when one of us put this theory to the test it was found that out of a clutch of six eggs, three failed to hatch, two produced badly deformed young, and one yielded a perfect hatchling—and this was the only egg to be turned, daily from day 20 to day 85.

It is now generally accepted that incubation temperature is influential in determining the sex of hatchlings of at least some reptile species. It has been found that tortoise eggs incubated at over 86°F (30°C) produce mainly females, while those kept below 82°F (28°C) yield a higher percentage of males.

An average incubation temperature is therefore 82°F to 86°F (28°C to 30°C).

High humidity does not seem to be a prerequisite of successful incubation, and the time of incubation may be from 55 days to 120 days or even more.

Rates of hatching may be affected by the fecundity of one or both parents, which is dependent on health, age and diet.

When ready to emerge, the juvenile pips a hole in the egg using the "caruncle," a small projection on its snout. This is a most critical time, for the need to breathe atmospheric air when the time arrives is an urgent one. The hatchling may now remain in the egg for about 24 hours, its occasional movements breaking more of the egg away. Eventually, it gathers the strength to crawl out.

The shell of the newly hatched juvenile is soft, and the plastron has a transverse crease where it was doubled up in the egg. This, and the swollen yolk sac on the plastron, may make locomotion difficult, but the condition is transitory; the crease disappears in about 48 hours and the yolk sac's contents are gradually absorbed into the system.

The little tortoise is now ready to feed, and here the real difficulties arise. The provision of a correctly balanced diet for adult tortoises has already been stressed, but the problems of feeding juveniles are infinitely more critical. If the diet is not appropriate to the needs of the baby, it is likely to grow into a stunted, deformed individual that, though fertile, may be physically incapable of mating or carrying eggs. The diet during the first few months of life is absolutely critical, and deformity resulting from dietary deficiency at this stage is irreversible. The common method used for raising hatchling tortoises for several years, which has proved eminently successful, is described in the following paragraphs.

The hatchlings are maintained in plastic trays measuring 16 by 12 by 3 inches (40 by 30 by 7.5 centimeters). They are sometimes kept in twos or threes and sometimes singly. The base of the tray is covered by a removable hygiene sheet similar to that used in bird cages, which gives the tortoise purchase in locomotion and helps to keep its claws short.

On a few occasions tortoises have been observed eating sand scuffed off the sheet. Some criticism has been leveled concerning possible dangers of ingesting the glue that binds the sand to the paper. However, we cannot confirm this supposition, and one of us has raised nearly 100 tortoises using this method.

Heat is provided in the form of 100-watt spot lamps suspended over the trays at a height from which a base temperature of 79°F (26°C) is obtained. These are left on day and night.

A 4-inch-wide strip of plywood is placed over one end of the tray as a shade area. Again contrary to accepted dogma, no ultraviolet radiation—natural or artificial—is provided. The hatchlings nevertheless develop well-shaped bodies and show very acceptable growth rates.

Drinking water is available at all times. The lids of plastic petri dishes prove ideal as water pots because they are shallow yet not easily tipped. Later, as the tortoises grow, the dishes have to be used in place of the lids.

Some hatchlings that are raised in captivity may exhibit deformities, among them a lumpy shell and hourglass constrictions at the carapace-plastron bridge. These deformities may well be related to an inadequate diet, particularly low levels of animal protein. It seems that although the tortoise is unlikely to consume vast amounts of meat in the wild, in captivity animal protein com-

The common turtle, or terrapin.

The painted turtle, *Chrysemys picta*.

pensates for the shortcomings of the less varied vegetable diet.

The following is a suitable weekly feeding for young tortoises:

MONDAY: Cabbage, cress, tomato, grated carrot. Flowers and foliage of native vegetation (e.g., dandelion, clover, vetch, buttercup). Animal protein: whole sprats, chopped

TUESDAY: Vegetables as above. Apple. Animal protein: canned dog food

WEDNESDAY: Rest day: no food

THURSDAY: Vegetables as above. Animal protein: canned dog food

FRIDAY: Vegetables as above. No animal protein

SATURDAY: Rest day: no food

SUNDAY: Vegetables as above. Apple. Animal protein: canned dog

© B. Kahl/Tetra

Finally, to dispel another myth, juvenile tortoises can be safely hibernated for two to three months if they have received adequate diets during their few months of life.

With regard to hibernation, tortoises should be packed away as their activity decreases and appetite wanes each fall. The exact time will depend on the geographic location, and may vary from year to year. A stout cardboard or wooden box three-quarters full of straw or shredded newspaper is ideal. This should have adequate ventilation holes and be stored somewhere at a steady cool temperature (e.g., in the basement or an unheated garage). Be sure that the tortoise cannot climb out of the box, and that rats and the like cannot get in. During the spring, the tortoise (as it awakes) should be given ready access to drinking water and a good, varied diet, and, if relevant, gradually reacclimated to outdoor conditions. Watch out for late frosts; it may be a good idea to bring the tortoise in each evening during the early spring.

Some of the more hardy North American box turtles (*Terrapene*) can be kept in a similar fashion to European land tortoises, although they require a more carnivorous diet and are probably less easy to hibernate successfully. They may require overwintering indoors or a hibernation period of a few weeks rather than months. If in doubt, consult your local turtle expert.

BREEDING AQUATIC TURTLES

Provided above are some details on the breeding of red-eared turtles and the European land tortoise. A few hints on the breeding of aquatic turtles are provided below.

If you keep adult specimens, you will quite naturally want to breed them. The most important prerequisite for this, apart from a first-rate feeding program, is a well-fitted aqua-terrarium, since aquatic turtles can be bred indoors. It is important that the individuals themselves be "compatible." It is not unusual to see turtles display a distinct aversion to a particular partner, while they immediately take to a replacement of the same—and this pair will soon proceed to courtship and mating.

food. Vitamin-mineral supplementation is given with all meals, and powdered cuttlebone, which is necessary with every meal if animal protein is not given, is provided twice weekly. Fruit is given sparingly. It must be noted that diet is dependent to some degree on the individual; not all tortoises eat all offered foods, nor do all grow at the same rate.

When a pair of turtles are well suited to one another, they will indulge in various courtship preliminaries almost constantly, though as a rule copulation itself takes place only in the evening. A water change prior to their being placed together may have a stimulating effect on them.

When females are ready to lay eggs they become noticeably restless. They take to the land and move around in an agitated fashion, often attempting to climb out of the tank. A female that is about to lay eggs may also return briefly to the water before leaving it once more, very unsettled. It often happens that she will dig holes in several places before she finds a place that is acceptable to her. Female turtles excavate their hollows laboriously with their hind legs. These hollows are vertical, pear-shaped holes, wider at the bottom than at the top. During the actual laying process, each emerging egg has its descent slowed as the female carefully guides it with her hind leg down into the hole or onto the rest of the clutch. Once the laying procedure is concluded, the hole is covered over and the earth patted down onto the eggs so that the spot under which the eggs are hidden will be difficult to recognize.

In large aqua-terrariums with a large land zone (soil temperature 79°F to 86°F [26°C to 30°C]), the eggs can be left in the nest hole. However, the clutch should be cordoned off with a close-meshed piece of wire netting to deter other females from digging in the same spot. This measure will also help to prevent the freshly hatched youngsters from diving straight into the water, where they may be looked on as fair game by the larger turtles—and eaten. However, the wire-netting cage must be big enough to offer the hatchlings sufficient room to move around freely. But if preferred—and this is probably a better approach—the eggs can be dug out after they have been laid and transferred to an "incubator" kept at a steady, warm temperature. Such incubators can be made from small fish tanks and a small-wattage light bulb or purchased from horticultural suppliers (incubators used for growing plant seedlings can be used as turtle incubators). It is often stated that when turtle eggs are moved for incubation, their exact orientation should be noted (by marking with a pen), as unnecessary movement of fertile eggs may result in embryo damage. The recent experience of some herpetologists now suggests that such specific reorientation is not always necessary.

When removed from the aqua-terrarium, the hard-shelled eggs should be gently embedded in moistened, but not too wet, peat. The eggs should be buried at a depth of 2 to 4 inches. In order to sterilize the peat, pour boiling water over it. Vermiculite can be used in place of peat. Excessive moisture must always be avoided.

The incubation temperature should be held steady in the region of 82°F to 86°F (28°C to 30°C), and hatching often occurs (depending on the species of turtle) after 70 to 100 days. Once out of their eggs, the hatchlings can be raised as described earlier in this chapter.

Although it is difficult to generalize, many of the commonly kept aquatic turtles mature at several years of age, and the males can often be distinguished by the longer claws on their front legs.

DISEASES AND DISEASE PREVENTION

Given proper care, most turtles are extremely hardy and long-lived. However, they may suffer from a number of ailments from time to time, and a few of the more common problems are outlined below. Cleanliness, a good, varied diet, and the correct tempera-

If you are keeping large turtles, your aqua-terrarium should probably not be this elaborate, as large chelonians may destroy the decorations.

EURAQUARIUM spa

© C. Andrews/Tetra

© B. Kahl/Tetra

ture conditions will go a long way toward preventing most diseases, but when in doubt about disease diagnosis and treatment, turtle keepers should always contact their local veterinarian.

NON-INFECTIOUS ILLNESSES

As a result of an incorrect diet with an inadequate supply of vitamins and minerals, including trace elements, turtles in captivity may suffer from an extensive range of symptoms of illness that can best be classed together as "deficiency syndromes."

Oedema of the eyelid

Species of the genera *Pseudemys, Chrysemys,* and to a lesser extent *Graptemys* are sometimes affected by oedema of the eyelid.

The typical manifestation of this illness is thickly swollen, oedematose eyelids that make it impossible for the animals to open their eyes, making it difficult for them to find food. In almost all cases, the Harderian gland, which largely encompasses the back of the eye, is also affected at the same time. In the more advanced stages, there is a heavy suppuration from the eyes, resulting ultimately in their utter ruin—if the animals have not already starved to death.

The cause of this complaint has been found to be vitamin A deficiency. In the initial stages the appropriate therapy lies in administering vitamin A either orally or, better still, via intramuscular injection. Simultaneous treatment with vitamin A ointment can be used to back up the healing process, signs of which become apparent after just a few days.

In the more advanced stages, the prospects of recovery are less good, because at this point it is also necessary to remove the case-

Graptemys flavimaculata, a particularly beautiful map turtle native to the southeastern United States.

Two specimens of the spur-thighed tortoise, *Testudo graeca*. The specimen on the left is a 14-month-old juvenile and the one on the right is an older tortoise with a deformed shell.

ous coating between the eyelid and the nictitating membrane, an operation that requires a great deal of skill.

Growth Deformities, or "Soft Shell"

There are a number of metabolic disturbances lumped together under this heading, many of which can be distinguished from one another only with some difficulty and which occur partly as a secondary phenomenon arising out of another complaint belonging to this disease "complex." The skeleton is most often affected. In the advanced stages, the carapace may soften and become deformed; there may occasionally also be signs of abnormal growth. The shell of such specimens can be depressed inwards in a most unnatural fashion. In young specimens this disease manifests itself as deformity of growth caused by insufficient deposition of mineral salts in the bones, whereas in older turtles the illness usually is manifest as a softening of the bones. The causes are generally held to be a lack of vitamin D, in particular D_3, or of sunlight (specifically the ultraviolet rays), as well as an incorrect ratio of calcium to phosphorus in the diet. This ratio should lie around the 1.2–1.5:1 mark, which can be supplied with any degree of assurance only with a very well-balanced composition, such as in veterinary diet supplements made for this very purpose, or by offering a very varied diet.

Where the proportion of phosphorus is very high—for example, ox heart at 1:28 or ox liver at 1:44—the bone tissue may be replaced by connective tissue, which can have disastrous effects for the turtle. It is therefore important to prevent the problem via a proper diet.

INFECTIOUS ILLNESSES AND BACTERIAL INFECTIONS

Turtles can harbor a range of bacteria in or on their bodies, and the common presence of *Salmonella* and similar bacteria in aquatic turtles highlights the need for sensible hygiene on the part of the turtle-keeper. It is fortunate, however, that the turtles are usually "carriers" of the organisms in question, without usually suffering from their effects. In contrast, other bacteria, such as the pathogens of tuberculosis in cold-blooded animals (*Mycobacterium* spp.), that can lead to pathological conditions in the lungs and other organs (e.g., the liver or the spleen) in turtles are rather uncommon. Turtles that appear to be askew when swimming and have trouble diving may be affected by some kind of infection of the lungs. Quite a wide range of pathogens may be responsible for this, including the above-mentioned mycobacteria. The infection can only be proven and identified, however, through the dissection of the animal in question, and successful treatment is difficult.

Respiratory Infections

Turtles can also fall ill with infections of the respiratory passages, which in the most unfavorable cases can develop into pneumonia. Pneumonia is caused by various microorganisms and it is mainly weaker animals who are attacked, especially if they stay in a draft that appears when aqua-terrariums are not properly arranged or are sited incorrectly.

The first indications of this disease are the aquatic turtle staying on land for long periods and not accepting food. Close observation of such animals shows that foam may form on the nostrils when breathing. Turtles in an advanced stage breathe with a whistling noise and often breathe only with a slightly opened mouth.

If such animals go into the water, an uncoordinated swimming motion is seen. Diving activities succeed only with great effort, and even then the animal quickly drifts back to the water surface.

Treatment at the advanced stage is unlikely to be successful. Sick animals can be put under an infrared lamp with a temperature range from 86°F to 90°F (30°C to 32°C), carefully avoiding overheating the "patients." It is also possible to let turtles inhale decongestant vapors. For this purpose Friars Balsam, for example, can be bought at a chemist's. This liquid, when added to hot water, forms a vapor. The bowl containing the Balsam-water mix is then placed in a covered container with the turtle for a few minutes, several times for a week or so. The bowl must be such that it cannot be upset by the turtle.

Vitamin and antibiotic injections from a vet may also be worthwhile, and the advice of a veterinarian may be particularly useful in this context. However, correct diet and steady temperatures are both vital in preventing pneumonia in turtles.

Ear Infections

Inflammation of the middle ear of turtles, which takes the form of a yellowish, cheesy plug building up in the ear, causing the membranes below the skin to bulge outwards, is caused by various organisms. To begin with, the vitality of the turtles is only slightly impaired, but they should be treated quickly or their general well-being will dete-

riorate rapidly and they may die. Treatment consists of a surgical operation performed by a veterinarian, followed by treatment with antibiotics.

Infection of the Shell

It is not unusual for deep, craterlike wounds to appear on the shells of water turtles, with the bones being severely affected as well. This eating away of the shell may be caused by a bacterium, although the pathogens for it have only rarely been isolated. Treatment with an antibacterial solution, consisting of the careful dabbing of the affected area using a clean tissue or cotton bud, can bring about a cure.

Mycotic Infections

Various types of fungi can cause infections both on the skin surface and in the internal organs of turtles. They are generally of little significance and, in the case of surface lesions, for instance, where a piece of horny carapace has become detached and revealed an infection, are simple to treat.

The best way for the amateur to treat such infections is to use daily baths in a solution of potassium permanganate. The turtles are bathed in this solution, which must be made up fresh each time and should have a light violet color, for a 10- to 20-minute period every day over a week or more. Another pos-

Regular monitoring of the growth of your turtle can be interesting and informative.

sible way to treat these infections is to paint the affected parts several times a day with an iodine-based antiseptic available from a vet. During treatment for this problem, the animals must be kept dry and allowed into the water only for brief periods for feeding.

PARASITES AND PROTOZOANS

Various types of protozoans occur in turtles. Of these only a few have any significance as real causes of disease. Without any doubt the most important of these are *Hexamita parva*, a flagellate organism, and the amoeba *Entamoeba invadens*.

Hexamita parva

Hexamita parva is a small flagellate that has 6 forward-pointing and 2 backward-pointing flagella. It is slender, only 8 to 10 microns long, and propels itself forward in rapid swimming movements. The flagellates colonize the kidneys and the urinary bladder—and occasionally the bile ducts—and cause a marked change in the infected animal's disposition. The affected individuals are lethargic, refuse food, and become very thin. Also, the feces are slimy. Death often results from this infection, which is transmitted via water. It can be treated by frequent bathing over a 2- to 3-week period using Emtryl (dimetridazole). Contact your local vet for more information.

Entamoeba invadens

Entamoeba invadens is an amoeba that is 15 to 20 microns in size and lives primarily as a harmless communal organism in the intestine. It is quite rare for turtles to suffer from amoebiasis, and when this does occur it is usually already weakened individuals, such as those that may have been kept under poor conditions at the dealers and during transport, that are affected. While these organisms represent minimal danger for the turtles, they are carried by the chelonians and, in cases where the turtles are kept in close proximity to other reptiles, especially snakes

and monitors, the amoeba can be transferred all too easily—and with devastating consequences. Reptiles such as lizards and snakes can succumb to the infection very quickly.

Entamoeba invadens colonizes the hindmost sections of the intestine and destroys the mucous membrane, leading to a bloody, crustlike coating. The amoeba can also be carried via the bloodstream into the liver, where large abscesses will then form. Individuals afflicted by this die after 3 to 6 weeks. At the start of their illness, the animals pass feces that are usually mixed with blood, but later the necrotic coating on the wall of the gut reduces the lumen to such an extent that the passage becomes blocked. The animals then become lethargic, sit with their mouth agape, either refuse food or regurgitate anything they do eat, and lose weight rapidly. Diagnosis is by identification of the amoeba in fresh feces or by dissection of the bodies of dead animals.

Treatment is problematic, but can be successful in the early stages. One form of treatment that has proved effective is oral administration of metronidazole (e.g., Flagyl) at a rate of up to 200 mg/kg of body weight per day over a period of a week. It is recommended that this be repeated after a break of a further two weeks. Your local vet can assist with this and related treatments.

The most important steps that can be taken to prevent the transmission of this organism are the maintenance of the best possible standards of hygiene and the observation of the following "rules":

1. Keep each newly acquired specimen in quarantine for several weeks before it is put in with other turtles.
2. Promptly remove any uneaten food; maintain hygienic tank conditions.
3. Have a postmortem carried out on any dead animals to establish the cause of death.
4. Thoroughly disinfect the turtle tank after any illness or death.
5. Disinfect any equipment used in boiling water.
6. Once animals have settled in, do not transfer them to other tanks.

Haemogregarines

In many water turtles coccidia of the genus *Haemogregarina* can be found in the blood as parasites. They are transmitted by leeches and usually occur only in animals that were caught in the wild; they cannot be transmitted in captivity.

These pathogens lead to death only in very exceptional cases. No treatment is known.

HELMINTHS ("WORMS")

Of the forms of parasites that are included in this group, namely trematodes, cestodes, and hematodes, only the last named are of any importance.

Trematodes (flukes)

Trematodes, which are also called flukes, have a rather complicated development cycle, often with snails serving as intermediate hosts. Because of this, the presence of trematodes in turtles kept in indoor tanks is unlikely. Trematodes live predominantly in the intestines, where they are harmless, though they can also colonize the lungs, the bile ducts in the liver, the gall bladder, the kidneys, and the ureter.

Diagnosis is by examining the feces for the tiny characteristic, shell-covered eggs. An infestation of trematodes can be treated with a one-off dose of Droncit (praziquantel) at a rate of 10 to 20 mg/kg of body weight, given orally.

The box turtles, *Terrapene* spp., are quite popular in North America. Shown here is an example of *Terrapene carolina,* a box turtle native to the eastern United States.

Tetra Archive

Cestodes (tapeworms)

Tapeworms live exclusively in the alimentary canal. They are rare in turtles and cannot be transmitted in captivity because of their complex life cycle. Their presence is diagnosed from tiny eggs in the feces.

Treatment is as for trematodes.

Nematodes (roundworms)

In turtles there are a number of species of these parasites, predominantly affecting the intestine. It takes a specialist to identify them with any certainty.

Diagnosis is usually on the grounds of typical eggs in the feces, occasionally accompanied by adult or juvenile nematodes.

The most straightforward method of deworming is by means of one of two oral preparations: Panacur (fenbendazole), a once-only treatment of 30 to 50 mg/kg of body weight; and Rintal (febantel), a once-only treatment of 30 to 50 mg/kg of body weight. It is recommended that treatment should be repeated after two weeks in order to eradicate any worms that have developed out of an earlier stage in the life cycle. Once again, your vet can help.

OTHER AILMENTS

Of the many and varied factors that influence the vitality of turtles and ultimately lead to severe illness there is one frequently occurring phenomenon that should be mentioned here: refusal to eat.

The reasons turtles refuse food may derive from one or a combination of factors, of which only a few will be discussed here. Unless one can succeed in persuading the animals to take food fairly quickly, they go into a rapid decline, suffer a marked weight loss, and finally die.

Loss of appetite may be caused by outside factors, such as the turtles in question being kept at too low a temperature or their tank being overstocked, but it can also occur in certain individuals after hibernation, in circumstances where the animal went into its winter rest period in a less than healthy state. It is also quite common for freshly imported animals, especially weakened individuals, to refuse food that is often unfamiliar to them.

In such cases intramuscular injection of water-soluble vitamin preparations usually brings about a rapid improvement. These preparations must contain the whole vitamin B complex and also contain vitamin A. The dosage depends upon the concentration of the mixtures to be used, and veterinary help and advice should be sought.

If the creature in question does not revert to its normal feeding pattern after this, one can assume there must be some other cause for the condition, such as a severe attack of intestinal parasites or a bacterial infection of the alimentary canal.

Whatever happens, do not let this set of potential problems put you off keeping turtles. Look after your turtles correctly, and you will probably never see any of these illnesses and ailments.

SOME COMMONLY KEPT AQUATIC TURTLES

Here is a summary of some useful information on a selection of commonly kept aquatic turtles. Females are generally larger than males and it is the maximum shell length of the adult female of each species that is referred to here. In addition to being smaller than the female, the mature males of many American turtles also have longer claws on their front legs.

Genus: *Chrysemys* (Painted turtles)

■ Species: *Chrysemys picta*
There are four known subspecies

Subspecies: *Chrysemys picta picta*
Distribution: Southeastern Canada and the eastern United States
Size: 7 inches (17.5 centimeters)

The carapace of this subspecies, dark brown as far as the edges, is not keeled and not serrated on the rear edge. The plates at the edge have red spots, both above and below. The rib and vertebral plates are arranged in practically regular transverse rows and have an ivory-colored stripe on their front edge. The head and limbs have a pretty pattern of yellow lined and flecked markings. The basic color of the plastron is yellow, with a large, dark and usually symmetrical figure along the central line.

In the wild these turtles live in quiet, slow-flowing or still stretches of water with plenty of vegetation both in the water and on the banks. They are fond of perching on drifting tree trunks and like to bathe in the sun. They are mainly carnivorous, but from time to time will eat soft plants. In captivity they are not impartial to eating lettuce, bananas, and other vegetables and fruits on occasion.

The temperature these turtles require depends largely upon the geographical area they come from. The same applies to any need for a winter rest or hibernation period, with the temperature lowered accordingly. The region of origin is the decisive factor in determining this, and your dealer may be able to give more precise information.

Subspecies: *Chrysemys picta belli*
Distribution: Southern and western Canada; western, southwestern, and central United States
Size: 10 inches (25 centimeters)

The unkeeled, unserrated, and very flat carapace is a shining olive-green in young specimens, but as the animal grows older this darkens, turning dark olive to olive-brown. In the juvenile stage there is also a raylike pattern in a yellowish-red to red shade to be seen. The plastron is orange to red. On it there is a dark pattern that has lateral outrunners running from points along the transverse lines. Head, neck, and limbs are a greenish-gray. In contrast to the head and neck, which display yellow line markings, the fore- and hind limbs, which are webbed and armed with powerful claws, are marked with red longitudinal lines or dots. This subspecies is one of the most beautiful of all turtles.

In captivity it is not easy to care for, as it constitutes the most delicate of the *Chrysemys* turtles.

Subspecies: *Chrysemys picta dorsalis*
Distribution: Southeastern United States
Size: 6 inches (15 centimeters)

This subspecies has a black carapace with an orange to yellow longitudinal stripe running along its middle. The plastron, reddish at the sides in young specimens, is whitish-yellow and unmarked. The color of the visible parts of the body is dark to black. Head and neck have a yellow pattern of streaks and flecks, while the limbs display orange-red stripes. The requirements of this subspecies are similar to those for *C. picta belli*, but it is more robust once it has settled in. Youngsters can prove difficult to raise.

One adult female kept by one of the authors for more than twenty years spent the period from May to September (in northern Europe) in an outdoor pond and regularly laid a batch of eggs in November and in January. These remained unfertilized because a male was not present.

Subspecies: *Chrysemys picta marginata*
Distribution: Southern Canada and eastern regions of the United States
Size: 8 inches (20 centimeters)

In this subspecies, the plates of the carapace are not arranged in transverse rows and the light coloring to the edges is often missing. The ventral shield, which is usually orange, has a broad, dark, longitudinal stripe without any lateral outrunners.

Genus: *Pseudemys* (Cooters, sliders, and red-ears)

With the exception of the species *Pseudemys terrapen*, all species of this genus occur only in North, Central, and South America. The method of keeping these turtles in aqua-terrariums is essentially the same, but they do have different temperature requirements, depending on their region of origin.

■ Species: *Pseudemys concinna* (River cooter)

The juveniles of this species have a deep green, keeled carapace with light yellow or orange-yellow hieroglyph-like markings.

These are replaced in older specimens by a dark olive to black coloring. The pale yellow plastron usually has some dark spots. The neck and head, as well as the limbs, have yellow parallel stripes running lengthwise along them on a dark gray background. They have webbing between the toes to aid swimming. The sharp claws on the toes are particularly long in sexually mature males.

This species lives principally in quiet rivers, lakes, and pools that have an abundance of vegetation in the water and on the banks. They are not fussy about their food. What is predominantly a carnivorous diet in the juveniles gradually changes to a preference for vegetable matter as the animals grow older.

Like all species of *Pseudemys,* these turtles are very fond of sunbathing. Care should be taken to cater to this habit. It is recommended that they be kept outside during the warmer months of the year. They do not need to hibernate. The air and water temperatures should be around 77°F (25°C) and must not be allowed to fall below 68°F (20°C).

There are six known subspecies.

Subspecies: *Pseudemys concinna concinna*
Distribution: Eastern United States, northeastern Mexico
Size: 13 inches (32.5 centimeters)

The spiny soft-shelled turtle, *Trionyx spiniferus,* is a shy, retiring turtle with a strong bite.

Subspecies: *Pseudemys concinna hieroglyphica*
Distribution: Southern United States
Size: 15 inches (38 centimeters)

Subspecies: *Pseudemys concinna hiltoni*
Distribution: Northwestern Mexico
Size: 15 inches (37.5 centimeters)

Subspecies: *Pseudemys concinna mobilensis*
Distribution: Southeastern United States
Size: 15 inches (37.5 centimeters)

This species is a favorite of turtle-keepers, as it is easily cared for.

Subspecies: *Pseudemys concinna suwanniensis*
Distribution: Southeastern United States
Size: 15 inches (37.5 centimeters)

In our experience, this turtle can be kept in captivity quite easily. It is the *Pseudemys* subspecies that grows the fastest. Over a period of 20 months, one specimen grew from a size of 1½ inches (3.75 centimeters) to 7½ inches (18.75 centimeters), without there being any evidence of deformities that one so often encounters in specimens that grow quickly.

Subspecies: *Pseudemys concinna texana*
Distribution: Southern United States, northeastern Mexico
Size: 13 inches (32.5 centimeters)

According to the literature, this species is said to eat no vegetable matter at all, but is otherwise kept in exactly the same way as the other subspecies.

■ Species: *Pseudemys dorbigni* (Brazilian turtle)
Distribution: Southern Brazil, Uruguay, northern Argentina
Size: 8 inches (20 centimeters)

This is a distinct species and does not form any recognized geographical subspecies. It can rightly be considered one of the most beautiful representatives of the genus, particularly in the juvenile stage. The gently arched carapace has a yellow barred pattern. The edging plates have a yellow central spot, surrounded by a black hem. The plastron displays a large, dark, highly branched figure that covers it almost completely. Behind the eyes there is a glowing orange fleck.

Tetra Archive

Neck and limbs are dark gray with yellowish-orange to yellow flecked or striped markings. This is the species whose range extends farthest to the south. The only way in which its requirements differ from the others is that it needs a higher temperature. On average, temperatures in both the air and water should be around 79°F (26°C). There should be no period of hibernation.

■ Species: *Pseudemys floridana* (southern turtle)

In the juvenile stage the plates of the green carapace are covered with a distinctive and eye-catching yellow-lined set of markings that soon disappears to make way for an olive to black coloring. A more or less noticeable, light longitudinal stripe remains visible only on the second dorsal plate. Another characteristic of all *floridana* subspecies is the steep, forward-sloping incline of the carapace, meaning that its greatest height is in front of the mid-point. The yellowish plastron has few spots, if any at all. The limbs are dark brown to black. This species has webbing between the toes and sharp claws.

This gregarious turtle is often encountered in groups of 20 to 30 individuals in its natural habitat. It likes to sunbathe together with other species of *Pseudemys* or *Graptemys* on floating tree trunks, small islands, or parts of the banks that are out of reach of predators. It is true that they belong among the species requiring plenty of warmth, but if as adults they are kept in the garden pond they will continue to take food at a water temperature of 64°F (18°C) and behave normally. The temperature at which they feel most at ease is probably around 77°F (25°C).

This species occurs in three subspecies.

Subspecies: *Pseudemys floridana floridana*
Distribution: Southeastern United States
Size: 16 inches (40 centimeters)

Subspecies: *Pseudemys floridana hoyi*
Distribution: Southern United States
Size: 16 inches (40 centimeters)

Subspecies: *Pseudemys floridana peninsularis*

Distribution: Southeastern United States
Size: 16 inches (40 centimeters)

———

■ Species: *Pseudemys grayi*
Distribution: Southern Mexico, Guatemala, El Salvador
Size: 14 inches (35 centimeters)

The basic coloring of the carapace is dark olive with a pattern similar to peacocks' "eyes." This is still visible in fully grown specimens. The yellowish-white plastron is lightly marbled. A characteristic feature of the species is a narrow, shiny orange-red stripe on the temples. The snout runs out to a point at the tip and the chewing surfaces of the upper jaw have ridges armed with strong teeth. The position of the nostrils—well below the tip of the snout—is a conspicuous feature. There is a light central stripe that forks backwards on the underside of the throat. The toes are equipped with pronounced webbing and have powerful claws.

Because this very appealing species is not well known and is rarely kept in captivity, there is little information available on it. The conditions it requires would probably be similar to those of the other *Pseudemys* species.

■ Species: *Pseudemys ornata*
There are three known subspecies of this turtle, the life-style of which is largely identical to that of other species of *Pseudemys*.

Subspecies: *Pseudemys ornata callirostris*
Distribution: Northern South America
Size: 14 inches (35 centimeters)

Subspecies: *Pseudemys ornata nebulosa*
Distribution: Northwestern Mexico
Size: 14 inches (35 centimeters)

Subspecies: *Pseudemys ornata ornata*
Distribution: Southern Mexico, Guatemala, Honduras, Nicaragua, Costa Rica, Panama
Size: 14 inches (35 centimeters)

The mostly dark olive carapace has on the plates not only a reticulated or striped set of markings, but also large, round, dark-edged eye patterns (peacocks' "eyes"). The ventral shield consists usually of light yellow lines that fade as the animal grows older. There are no other markings. The nostrils are positioned well below the tip of the snout. The light longitudinal stripes on the throat do not fork and stretch forward as far as the edge of the lower jaw. This subspecies possesses strong claws and has broad webbing between its toes.

■ Species: *Pseudemys rubriventris* (red-bellied turtle)
There are four subspecies of this turtle, and their requirements in terms of food and living conditions are the same as for the other species and subspecies of *Pseudemys*.

Subspecies: *Pseudemys rubriventris nelsoni*
Distribution: Southeastern United States, principally Florida
Size: 14 inches (35 centimeters)

Subspecies: *Pseudemys rubriventris alabamensis*
Distribution: Southeastern United States
Size: 14 inches (35 centimeters)

Subspecies: *Pseudemys rubriventris bangsi*
Distribution: Northeastern United States
Size: 14 inches (35 centimeters)

Subspecies: *Pseudemys rubriventris rubriventris*
Distribution: Eastern United States
Size: 16 inches (40 centimeters)

The carapace of this subspecies is brown to black and serrated or notched at the rear, and there are red to yellow markings. The plastron, at least at the edge, is red or reddish. Head, neck, and limbs are dark olive and have yellow striped markings. This species possesses sharp claws and broad webbing between the toes.

This and the other subspecies are rarely kept in aqua-terrariums, because they are not often on sale at dealers' shops.

■ Species: *Pseudemys scripta*
This species has four separate subspecies.

They are all beautifully marked creatures, especially when young.

Subspecies: *Pseudemys scripta elegans* (red-eared slider)
Distribution: Central and eastern United States
Size: 16 inches (40 centimeters)

The relatively flat carapace is a shiny green color in young specimens. As the animal gets older this turns to an olive or yellow-brown color, but still shows mottled patterns that can vary enormously. The peacock's "eye" of the edge plates later becomes blurred. The gleaming red fleck on either side of the temples makes this subspecies particularly striking. Head, neck, and limbs bear white to light green striations on a grayish-green background. It has very sharp claws and the toes are equipped with strong webbing. This subspecies is the most widely distributed of all in the United States, and occurs in all types of waters except cold mountain streams. It is without doubt the species of aquatic turtle that is most frequently kept in captivity. For purposes of keeping it in the home, and above all for outdoor purposes, it would be a great advantage to the amateur to know which climatic zone his particular specimens came from, but this information is seldom available. This turtle keeps predominantly to the water, leaving it only to sunbathe and to lay eggs, and it is not at all fussy about its food, though it should be noted that it shows an increasing preference for vegetable matter as it grows older. This subspecies is quite easy to breed, but people do not often attempt to breed them because they are so easy to obtain through the trade (where they are often bred on "turtle farms").

Subspecies: *Pseudemys scripta gaigeae*
Distribution: Southern United States to northern Mexico
Size: 10 inches (25 centimeters)

Subspecies: *Pseudemys scripta scripta*
Distribution: Eastern and northeastern United States
Size: 11 inches (27.5 centimeters)

This subspecies is a trouble-free subject for keeping in captivity, and is therefore especially recommended.

Subspecies: *Pseudemys scripta troostli*
Distribution: Eastern United States
Size: 10 inches (25 centimeters)
This subspecies can be distinguished from *Pseudemys scripta elegans*—to which it is very similar, apart from the smaller adult size—by virtue of the fleck on both sides of the temples being a glowing yellow, as opposed to a glowing red in *P.s. elegans*.

■ Species: *Pseudemys terrapen*
There are seven known subspecies of this turtle, though they are only rarely kept by amateurs because they are practically never available through pet dealers. However, the method of keeping them is no different from that used for the other *Pseudemys* species. The temperatures they require are lower than would seem to be suggested by their natural distribution range. The subspecies are listed below without further detail. They all are found on Caribbean islands.

Subspecies: *Pseudemys terrapen decorata*
Distribution: Antilles, Haiti, Ile de Vache
Size: 8 inches (20 centimeters)

Subspecies: *Pseudemys terrapen granti*
Distribution: Grand Cayman Island
Size: 10 inches (25 centimeters)

Subspecies: *Pseudemys terrapen malonei*
Distribution: Bahamas, Great Inagua Island
Size: 8 inches (20 centimeters)

Subspecies: *Pseudemys terrapen rugosa*
Distribution: Cuba, Isle of Pines
Size: 10 inches (25 centimeters)

Subspecies: *Pseudemys terrapen stejnegeri*
Distribution: Puerto Rico, Vieques Island
Size: 10 inches (25 centimeters)

Subspecies: *Pseudemys terrapen terrapen*
Distribution: Jamaica
Size: 10 inches (25 centimeters)

Subspecies: *Pseudemys terrapen vicina*
Distribution: Eastern Hispaniola, San Domingo
Size: 10 inches (25 centimeters)

Genus: *Graptemys* (Map turtles)
Six species can be distinguished within the genus *Graptemys*, but their lifestyle and the methods used for keeping them are similar to those for the general *Pseudemys* and *Chrysemys*.

One noticeable morphological feature of this genus is the considerably smaller size of the fully grown males. The sizes quoted for both the species and the subspecies relate only to female specimens.

■ Species: *Graptemys barbouri*
Distribution: Southeastern United States
Size: 11 inches (27.5 centimeters)

■ Species: *Graptemys geographica* (common map turtle)
Distribution: Southeastern Canada and northern United States
Size: 11 inches (27.5 centimeters)

■ Species: *Graptemys kohnii*
Distribution: Central to southern United States
Size: rarely up to 10 inches (25 centimeters)

In the juvenile stages there is a fine, reticulated pattern on the light brown carapace,

The snapping turtle, *Chelydra serpentina*, which is not a truly suitable subject for the amateur turtle-keeper, requires a diet of meat, fish, and some vegetable matter.

but this is soon lost. The rear edge is deeply serrated. A keel runs along the center with backward-pointing bumps that are dark brown to black at the tips. The plastron is light and displays a dark figure along the central line with lateral outrunners stretching out along the joins in the shield; this pattern disappears in older specimens.

There is a glowing yellow stripe running backward from the tip of the snout along the middle of the grayish-brown head. A yellow strip coming from the back of the head forms a surround to the rear part of the eye, ending below the middle part of it. The neck and limbs are also gray-brown with numerous light yellow longitudinal stripes. The toes are connected by large webs and bear sharp claws. This species is found in slow-flowing waters, lakes, ponds, and pools that contain plenty of vegetation.

Despite popular opinion, the map turtle, *Graptemys kohnii*, is relatively hardy, at least as an adult.

In the literature it is described as having particularly high temperature requirements, but our experience does not bear this out. *Graptemys kohnii* can even survive the winter in the open air pond—often when it even has an ice cover. Animals kept in this way start sunning themselves in early March when the water temperature is only 50°F (10°C), and the air temperature reaches 57°F (14°C). In their feeding and other requirements *Graptemys kohnii* is similar to the above-described species of other genera as well as to the other *Graptemys* species and subspecies. This species makes a pleasant subject that does not lose its natural shyness even after years of captivity. This species is particularly amenable in its attitude towards other turtles.

■ Species: *Graptemys oculifera*
Three subspecies are known. All of them have particularly beautiful markings on their shells and would be suitable aquaterrarium subjects because of their small size. However, they are only rarely encountered in pet shops.

Subspecies: *Graptemys oculifera flavimaculata*
Distribution: Southeastern United States
Size: Like *Graptemys oculifera flavimaculata* this subspecies grows to only 6 inches (15 centimeters) in length

Subspecies: *Graptemys oculifera nigrinoda*
Distribution: Southeastern United States
Size: The smallest of the three subspecies, with a maximum size of only 5 inches (12.5 centimeters)

Subspecies: *Graptemys oculifera oculifera*
Distribution: Southeastern United States
Size: Of all the turtles mentioned so far, this is probably the smallest, with a maximum length of 6 inches (15 centimeters)

■ Species: *Graptemys pseudographica* (false map turtles)

This species has four subspecies.

Subspecies: *Graptemys pseudogeographica ouachitensis*

Distribution: Central United States
Size: 10 inches (25 centimeters)

Subspecies: *Graptemys pseudographica pseudographica*
Distribution: Northern and central United States
Size: 10 inches (25 centimeters)

The appearance of this subspecies is similar to that of *Graptemys kohnii* but can be distinguished from it by the fact that the bow-shaped stripe running around its eye finishes at the top of the eye.

Subspecies: *Graptemys pseudographica sabinensis*
Distribution: Southern United States
Size: 8 inches (20 centimeters)

Subspecies: *Graptemys pseudographica versa*
Distribution: Southern United States
Size: 7 inches (17.5 centimeters)

■ Species: *Graptemys pulchra*
Distribution: Southeastern United States
Size: 7 inches (17.5 centimeters)

Genus: *Trionyx* (soft-shelled turtles)

■ Species: *Trionyx spiniferus* (spiny soft-shelled turtle)
Distribution: Southern North America
Size: 16 inches (40 centimeters)

Turtles of this subspecies have a soft, brown-green, putty-like shell. They spend almost all their time in the water, and require a temperature of around 77°F to 86°F (25°C to 30°C). They are quick-tempered and have a nasty bite. A meat and fish diet is best. *Trionyx ferox* (the Florida soft-shell) and some Old World species are also available from time to time.

Genus: *Kinosternon* (mud turtles)

Two species are most often available, and they are particularly aquatic in their habits. They frequently remain very shy in captivity. The diet should consist of a variety of meat and fish items, including worms and

insects. A temperature of 77°F (25°C) is adequate.

■ Species: *Kinosternon subrubrum* (common mud turtle)
Distribution: Eastern United States
Size: 4 inches (10 centimeters)

■ Species: *Kinosternon flavescous* (yellow mud turtle)
Distribution: North America
Size: 6 inches (15 centimeters)

The former species has a paler shell than the latter. Both have hinged shells, enabling them to close up tightly after withdrawing their head and legs. If threatened, they can produce an unpleasant smell and, despite their small size, deliver a painful bite.

Genus: *Mauremys*

■ Species: *Mauremys caspica* (Spanish "terrapin" or Caspian turtle)
Distribution: Mediterranean Europe to Middle East
Size: 8 inches (20 centimeters)

This species is very common in parts of southern Europe. It has rather dull olive or gray coloration (especially when adult). When young it requires a temperature of around 77°F (25°C), although once adult it can live in outdoor enclosures in the summer. A good, varied diet including plant and animal material is required.

Genus: *Cuora* (Asiatic box turtles)

■ Species: *Cuora amboiensis* (and others)
Distribution: Southeast Asia
Size: 8 inches (20 centimeters)

An attractive aquatic turtle with a brown carapace and a brown and yellow-striped head. Because of the hinged plastron, this turtle can withdraw completely into his box-like shell. This species prefers a temperature in the range of 77°F to 86°F (25°C to 30°C) and plenty of vegetable matter in the diet. This turtle likes to spend some time out of the water.

BIBLIOGRAPHY

Alderton, David, *Turtles and Tortoises of the World.* New York: Facts on File, 1988.

Bjorndal, Karen A. (ed.) *Biology and Conservation of Sea Turtles.* Washington, D.C.: Smithsonian Institution Press, 1982.

Bustard, H. Robert. *Sea Turtles: Their Natural History and Conservation.* New York: Taplinger Publishing Co., 1972.

Carr, Archie. *Handbook of Turtles: The Turtles of the United States, Canada and Baja California.* Ithaca, NY: Comstock Publishing Assoc., a division of Cornell University Press, 1952.

_____. *The Reptiles.* Alexandria, Va.: Time-Life Books, 1977.

_____. *So Excellent a Fish: A Natural History of Sea Turtles.* Garden City, N.Y.: Doubleday & Co., 1973, rev. 1977.

Cobb, Jo. *A Complete Introduction to Turtles and Terrapins.* Neptune City, N.J.: TFH Publications, 1987.

Ernst, Carl H., and Barbour, Roger W. *Turtles of the United States.* Lexington, Ky.: University Press, 1972.

Gibbons, Whit. *Their Blood Runs Cold: Adventures With Reptiles and Amphibians.* University, Ala.: The University of Alabama Press, 1977.

Holling, Holling Clancy. *Minn of the Mississippi.* Boston: Houghton Mifflin, 1951.

Jocher, Willy. *Turtles for Home and Garden.* Neptune City, N.J.: TFH Publications, 1973.

Nicholls, Richard E. *The Running Press Book of Turtles.* Philadelphia: Running Press, 1977.

Obst, Fritz J. *Turtles, Tortoises and Terrapins.* New York: St. Martin's Press, 1986.

Pope, Clifford. *Turtles of the United States and Canada.* New York: Knopf, 1939.

Pritchard, Peter C.H. *Encyclopedia of Turtles.* Neptune City, N.J.: TFH Publications, 1979.

Reidman, Sarah R., and Ross William. *Turtles: Extinction or Survival?* New York: Abelard-Schuman, 1974.

Rudloe, Jack. *Time of the Turtle.* New York: Knopf, 1979.

Smith, Hobart M., and Edmund D. Brodie, Jr. *Reptiles of North America: A Guide to Field Identification.* New York: Golden Press, 1982.

Zappalorti, Robert T. *The Amateur Zoologist Guide to Turtles and Crocodilians.* Harrisburg, Pa.: Stackpole Books, 1976.

FURTHER READING

Books

Alderton, D. *A Petkeeper's Guide to Reptiles and Amphibians.* London: Salamander, 1986.

Arnold, E.N., and J.B. Burton. *A Field Guide to Reptiles and Amphibians of Britain and Europe.* San Francisco: Collins Publishers, 1978.

Breen, J. *Encyclopedia of Reptiles and Amphibians.* Neptune, N.J.: TFH Publications Inc., 1974.

Conant, R. *A Field Guide to Reptiles and Amphibians of Eastern North America.* Boston: Houghton Mifflin Co., 1975.

Echternacht, A. *How Reptiles and Amphibians Live.* New York: Elsevier Science Publishing Co. Inc., 1977.

Jackson, O., and J. Cooper. *Diseases of the Reptilia.* San Diego: Academic Press Inc., 1981.

Mattison, C. *The Care of Reptiles and Amphibians.* London: Blandford, 1983.

Palmer, J. *Reptiles and Amphibians.* London: Blandford, 1983.

Porter, K. *Herpetology.* Philadelphia: WB Saunders Company, 1972.

Pritchard, P. *Encyclopedia of Turtles.* Neptune, N.J.: TFH Publications Inc., 1979.

Robinson, D. *Tortoises, Terrapins, and Turtles,* Edinburgh: Bartholomew, 1976.

Schmidt, K., and R. Inger. *Living Reptiles of the World.* London: Hamish Hamilton, 1965.

Stebbins, R. *A Field Guide to Western Reptiles and Amphibians.* Boston: Houghton Mifflin, 1966.

Magazines

Fishkeeping magazines—for example, *Aquarist and Pondkeeper* and *Practical Fishkeeping* from England, and *Tropical Fish Hobbyist* from the United States—often carry articles on reptiles and are useful sources of information on suppliers of livestock, live food, equipment, and other accessories.

SOURCES FOR INFORMATION

Turtle and Wildlife Organizations

California Turtle and Tortoise Club
P.O. Box 90252
Los Angeles, CA 90009

Caribbean Conservation Corp.
P.O. Box 2866
Gainesville, FL 32602

Center for Marine Conservation
1725 DeSales St., N.W.
Washington, D.C. 20036

Desert Tortoise Preserve Committee, Inc.
P.O. Box 453
Ridgecrest, CA 94133

Earth Island Institute
300 Broadway
San Francisco, CA 94133

Freshwater Turtles and Land Tortoise Specialists Group
(affiliated with the International Union for the Conservation of Nature—IUCN):

Michael Klemens, director of global program
Department of Herpetology and Icthyology
American Museum of Natural History
Central Park West at 79th St.
New York, NY 10024

Durrel Institute of Conservation and Ecology
University of Kent
Canterbury, Kent, United Kingdom CT27NY

Florida Audubon Society
1101 Audubon Way
Maitland, FL 32751

Greenpeace International
1436 U St., N.W.
Washington, DC 20009

HEART (Ridley Turtles)
P.O. Box 681231
Houston, TX 77268-1231

National Wildlife Federation
1400 16th St., N.W.
Washington, DC 20036-2266

New York Turtle and Tortoise Society
365 Pacific Street
Brooklyn, NY 11217

Sea Turtle Center
P.O. Box 634
Nevada City, CA 95959

World Wildlife Fund and The Conservation Foundation
1250 24th St., N.W.
Washington, DC 20037

I N D E X